W9-BOO-204

DATE DUE			

∠99-217

988.3   Lieberg, Carolyn S.
LIE

          Suriname

Chicago Southwest Christian Schools
OAK LAWN BUILDING
10110 SOUTH CENTRAL AVENUE
Oak Lawn, Illinois 60453

**SOUTHWEST CHICAGO
CHRISTIAN SCHOOLS**

848502 02396 02510B 04211E   004

ATLANTIC OCEAN

CARIBBEAN SEA

MARTINIQUE
BARBADOS

PUNTA DE GALLINAS
Barranquilla   Maracaibo   La Guaira   TRINIDAD AND TOBAGO
Cartagena   Valencia   CARACAS   Port of Spain
Panama   Mérida   Ciudad Bolívar   Georgetown   Paramaribo
VENEZUELA   GUYANA   Cayenne
ISLA DEL COCO   Medellín   BOGOTÁ   Boa Vista do   SURINAME   FR. GUIANA
(Costa Rica)   Nevado del Tolima   Rio Branco   GUIANA HIGHLANDS
ISLA DE   17,110   COLOMBIA   Cerro Cutú
MALPELO   7,990
(Colombia)   Quito   Cotopaxi   ILHA DE MARAJÓ   ROCEDOS SÃO PEDRO
ARCHIPIÉLAGO DE COLÓN   ECUADOR   19,347   Equator   E SÃO PAULO
(GALÁPAGOS ISLANDS)   Guayaquil   Chimborazo   Manaus   Belém   São Luís   (Brazil)
(Ec.)   20,561   (Manáos)   (Pará)   (Maranhão)
Iquitos   Rio Amazonas   ARQUIPÉLAGO
Leticia   Rio Negro   Fortaleza   FERNANDO DE NORONHA
Rio Solimões (Amazonas)   (Ceará)   (Brazil)
Chiclayo   Rio Branco   CABO DE SÃO ROQUE
Trujillo   Pôrto   Natal
Nevs. Huascarán   Velho   João Pessoa (Paraíba)
22,205   B R A Z I L   RECIFE (Pernambuco)
PERU   Maceió
LIMA   CHAPADA DE   SERRA DO PIAUÍ
Callao   Cuzco   MATO GROSSO   Salvador
Volcán Misti   Cuiabá   Brasília   (Bahia)
19,098   Diamantina
Arequipa   La Paz   BOLIVIA
Mollendo   Nev. Illimani   Sucre   Belo Horizonte
21,151   Potosí   Vitória
Iquique   GRAN CHACO   Bandeira
ANDES   PARAGUAY   SÃO PAULO   CABO FRIO
Antofagasta   Salta   Asunción   Santos   RIO DE JANEIRO
Tropic of Capricorn   Cerro Azufre (Copiapó)   Tucumán
ISLA DE SAN FÉLIX   22,547   Corrientes   Florianópolis
ISLA DE SAN AMBROSIO   Copiapó   Santa Fe   Salto
Coquimbo   Córdoba   Pôrto Alegre
Cerro Aconcagua   Rosario   URUGUAY
22,831   Mendoza   Rio Grande
Valparaíso   BUENOS AIRES
SANTIAGO   MONTEVIDEO
ISLAS DE JUAN FERNÁNDEZ   La Plata
(Chile)   PAMPAS
Concepción   A R G E N T I N A
Valdivia   Bahía Blanca
Puerto Montt   Viedma
ISLA DE   Golfo San Matías
CHILOÉ
ARCHIPIÉLAGO   Comodoro Rivadavia
DE LOS CHONOS   Monte Valentín   Golfo San Jorge
11,314
WELLINGTON   FALKLAND IS.
HANOVER   (ISLAS MALVINAS)
Río Gallegos   (Br.)
Punta Arenas   Stanley
DESOLACIÓN   Estrecho de Magallanes
Mt. Sarmiento   TIERRA DEL FUEGO
8,100   ISLA DE LOS ESTADOS
CABO DE HORNOS
(CAPE HORN)

PACIFIC OCEAN

ATLANTIC OCEAN

Drake Passage

SOUTH GEORGIA
(Falkland Is.)

SOUTH
SANDWICH
ISLANDS
(Falkland Is.)

SOUTH SHETLAND
ISLANDS
(B.A.T.)   JOINVILLE
ANTARCTIC   JAMES ROSS
PENINSULA
Antarctic Circle

SOUTH ORKNEY IS.
(B.A.T.)

CENTRAL AMERICA

Longitude West of Greenwich

3-5-I

Relief		
Meters		Feet
3050		10 000
1525		5000
610		2000
305		1000
0	Sea Level	0
152.5		500
1525		5000
3050		10 000
6100		20 000

Map from Goode's World Atlas,
© 1995 by Rand McNally, 94-S-267

988.3
LIE
L99-217
$23.96
6/99

Enchantment of the World

SURINAME

By Carolyn S. Lieberg

Consultant for Suriname: George I. Blanksten, Ph.D., Professor Emeritus of Political Science, Northwestern University, Evanston, Illinois

Consultant for Reading: Robert L. Hillerich, Ph.D., Professor Emeritus, Bowling Green State University; Consultant, Pinellas County Schools, Florida

Chicago ... Christian Schools
OAK LAWN BUILDING
10110 SOUTH CENTRAL AVENUE
Oak Lawn, Illinois 60453

CP CHILDRENS PRESS ®
CHICAGO

A gold chain, watch, and umbrella dress up the typical attire of this Saramaccan man.

Project Editor: Mary Reidy
Design: Margrit Fiddle
Photo Research: Feldman & Associates, Inc.

Library of Congress Cataloging-in-Publication Data

Lieberg, Carolyn S.
    Suriname / by Carolyn S. Lieberg.
        p.   cm.—(Enchantment of the world)
    Includes index.
    Summary: Discusses the geography, history, government, economics, people, and culture of the smallest independent country of South America.
    ISBN 0-516-02638-0
    1. Suriname—Juvenile literature. [1. Suriname.]
I. Title. II. Series.
F2408.5.L54   1995   95-2692
988.3—dc20   CIP
                                                    AC

Copyright © 1995 by Childrens Press®, Inc.
All rights reserved. Published simultaneously in Canada.
Printed in the United States of America.
1 2 3 4 5 6 7 8 9 10 R 04 03 02 01 00 99 98 97 96 95

Picture Acknowledgments
AP/Wide World Photos: 45, 47, 49
The Bettmann Archive: 26 (2 photos)
D. Donne Bryant Stock: © James D. Nations, Cover inset, 67, 79 (top left), 96 (left)
Courtesy of Conservation International: 18 (2 photos), 66 (right)
© Victor Englebert: 9, 40, 78 (left), 91
North Wind Picture Archives: 22 (2 photos), 23, 29
Chip and Rosa Maria de la Cueva Peterson: Cover, 6, 10, 12, 15 (top), 20, 21, 28, 31, 50, 59, 63, 64, 66 (left), 72 (2 photos), 73, 75 (2 photos), 76, 78 (right), 82, 92 (top right and bottom), 96 (right), 101 (bottom), 106 (top and bottom left), 122
Photri: 43, 76 (bottom), 79 (top right), 94
© Porterfield/Chickering: 24, 32 (2 photos), 33, 36, 88
Root Resources: © Jane P. Downton, 11, 15 (bottom right), 79 (bottom), 97, 106 (bottom right)
Tom Stack & Associates: © Wendy Shattil/Bob Rozinski, 16 (top); © Roy Toft, 17 (left)
SuperStock International, Inc.: 102; © Kurt Scholz, 61; © Hubertus Kanus, 62
UPI/Bettmann Newsphotos: 38, 42, 44
Valan: © Anthony Scullion, 15 (bottom left); © Prof. R. C. Simpson, 16 (bottom left); © John Cancalosi, 16 (bottom right), 17, 100; © Karl Weidmann, 81; © Jeff Foott, 83; © Maslowski, 84; © Jane K. Hugessen, 84 (inset); © Ken Cole, 98; © J. A. Wilkinson, 99 (left); © K. Ghani, 103
Viesti Associates, Inc.: © Martha Cooper, 4, 5, 34, 48, 55, 57 (2 photos), 58, 68, 69, 70, 85 (2 photos), 86, 89, 92 (top left), 107, 108
Visuals Unlimited: © Kjell B. Sandved, 99 (right); © John D. Cunningham, 101 (top)
Len W. Meents: Maps on 81, 83
Courtesy Flag Research Center, Winchester, Massachusetts 01890: Flag on back cover
Cover: Suriname rain forest
Cover inset: Paramaribo, Suriname

Village women prepare food for their families.

TABLE OF CONTENTS

Albina, on the Maroni River, lies on the border with French Guiana.

Chapter 1

THE LAND CALLED SURINAME

LOCATION AND BORDERS

The country of Suriname is one of three small countries on the northeastern shoulder of South America. It is the smallest independent country on the continent. Suriname rests between Guyana on the west and French Guiana on the east. Before gaining its independence from the Netherlands in 1975, Suriname was called Dutch Guiana. The three countries are part of a region called the Guianas, which is from an Amerindian word meaning "we who deserve respect." (The Amerindians are the American Indians—the native people of Suriname.) The Guianas region is bordered by water—the Amazon River on the south, the Orinoco and Negro Rivers in the west, and the Atlantic Ocean to the north and east. The area includes a northern section of Brazil and the eastern edge of Venezuela.

The border between Suriname and Brazil is just above the equator, and a line drawn from Suriname's center straight toward the North Pole leads directly over the Atlantic Ocean to the eastern reaches of Newfoundland.

As well as a centuries-old connection to the Netherlands, or Holland as it also is called, Suriname is linked to the Caribbean Islands. This chain of islands begins south of the tip of Florida, curves out like a backward C, and ends north of Venezuela, the country west of Guyana. Though the Caribbean Islands are not quite "next door" to Suriname, they share a history of settlement by Europeans, the importation of African slaves, and a reliance on ships for both transportation and trade. These features contribute to the cultural and economic interests that are shared by Suriname and the rest of the Caribbean community.

Suriname has an area of 63,037 square miles (163,266 square kilometers) and is about the size of the state of Washington or the North African country of Tunisia. Its shape is rather square, but its zigzags and curves make it seem to be rushing west. Three of its borders—eastern, western, and southern—are defined by winding rivers. Both Guyana to the west and French Guiana to the east dispute the precise location of the countries' shared borders. The dispute has grown violent at times because the land contains valuable minerals and will bring money to those who mine it.

The northern boundary of Suriname is, of course, on the Atlantic Ocean and is composed primarily of mud banks, swamp, and some sand drifts.

THE LAND

A miniature version of Suriname seen from above would display a country that is mostly lush and green. Next to the ocean is an area called the coastal plain, which extends inland from 10 miles (16 kilometers) on the east edge of the country to 50 miles

An aerial view of the rain forest

(80 kilometers) in the west. Most of this area is at sea level, which accounts for the swamps. Next comes a wider, slightly elevated strip of intermediate plain whose width varies from 30 miles (48 kilometers) in the east to 40 miles (64 kilometers) in the west. At this level, scattered sandy savannas bear only sparse vegetation. South of these fanlike plains, the mountainous rain forests begin to rise gradually toward the Wilhelmina Mountains, where Juliana Top reaches 4,200 feet (1,280 meters), Suriname's highest elevation.

In the center of the country is a chain of mountains called the Van Asch Van Wijk range that runs south to the Tumac-Humac Mountains on the Brazilian border. The largest lake in the country is Blommestein Lake, located in the east-central part of the nation. It was created when a dam was built to provide electrical power.

The geology of Suriname yielded a minor gold rush from 1880 to 1910. In recent decades the discovery of bauxite has led to a major export business.

The Marowijne River

Rain forests cover about 75 percent of the country. Several exotic woods are cut from the forests to be exported as timber, but some large areas have been left alone by developers.

The country is divided into eight districts: Brokopondo, Commewijne, Coronie, Marowijne, Nickerie, Para, Saramacca, and Suriname.

RIVERS

The coastal plain, where most of the Surinamese live, accounts for about 16 percent of the country's area. Seven major rivers that empty into the Atlantic Ocean cut across the land. It is no surprise that the largest cities of Suriname are located on the banks of these rivers, where trading and other business can be conducted easily. The main port and largest city, Paramaribo, is

Ships in the harbor at Paramaribo

also Suriname's capital, about fourteen miles (twenty-three kilometers) up the Suriname River from the Atlantic Ocean. The city was originally settled at that distance from the ocean to help protect it from pirates.

The other main rivers are the Courantyne, the Nickerie, the Coppename, the Saramacca, the Commewijne, and the Maroni.

The winding rivers feed the lush landscape of Suriname. They travel down the declining elevation, sometimes moving slowly and at other times rushing over falls and terraces to reach the Atlantic Ocean in the north. Surinamese have built many channels to get from one river to another. Water travel is by far the most common, most efficient way to move around the coastal plain. The country has 2,794 miles (4,496 kilometers) of navigable waterways and about twice that distance in roads, both paved and unpaved.

Birds gather on a tidal marsh in the province of Nickerie.

THE COASTAL SWAMPS

Suriname's coast is 226 miles (364 kilometers) long. The condition of the coast is determined by deposits from the rivers. The dominating swampy areas are interrupted by areas of higher terrain called beach ridges and also by large mud banks. These ridges and mud banks creep westward under the power of wind and ocean currents.

Most of the sand and soil along this stretch has been carried from elsewhere by the ocean, and the shoreline is slowly though constantly changing. The many smaller rivers do not have currents strong enough to flow directly into the ocean. Instead, the ocean currents push the muddy waters of the rivers in a westerly direction, which helps create the swampy areas along the coast. Something else that helps create swamps is clay, which prevents water from draining. Over the years, some clay has been brought north from the Amazon River by currents and wind, and it has settled into gullies and old riverbeds.

Many sections of the sea level area have been changed by people. In the 1600s the first lasting settlements by Europeans succeeded because the Europeans used African people as slaves. The slaves did the backbreaking work of creating plantations by building dikes to keep out the water. Before importing slaves, the Europeans attempted to enslave people from the native tribes, but the Amerindians resisted and escaped to the rain forests. The imported Africans tried this same way of escaping and it worked for many. Today many of their descendants live in rain-forest villages.

Although the land that is now Suriname was traded back and forth among European countries, it is interesting that such a wet area eventually became a colony of the Netherlands. The capital of this European country is Amsterdam, a city that relies on dikes to prevent its flooding because one-fifth of it is built on land that is below sea level. Waterways are as common in Amsterdam as boulevards are in cities of other countries.

CLIMATE

A combination of equatorial location, a high amount of moisture, and global winds contributes to the climate of Suriname. The thick rain forests reflect the fact that the country's rainfall is plentiful and nearly constant.

Suriname has four seasons, two wet and two dry. Nine months contain the two most dramatic seasons, and three months echo a lighter version of them. The long rainy season is from April to August, followed by a long dry season from August to November.

A shorter, less rainy wet season extends from December to February and a shorter, rather dry one follows, from February to March.

Rainfall is greatest in the mountains in the south and varies along the coast. The western area receives 76 inches (193 centimeters) annually; Paramaribo, in the eastern half of the country, receives 95 inches (241 centimeters) a year. This is about three times the amount of rain that falls in Seattle, Washington, each year.

The humidity in such a climate is high, but Suriname's location on the globe means that trade winds constantly blow off the Atlantic Ocean. These winds are strongest along the coastal plain and they diminish in the interior. Suriname is too far south to be affected by the damaging hurricane winds that seasonally rack the Caribbean Islands.

The temperature range is narrow year-round. In the daytime, it varies from 73 degrees Fahrenheit (23 degrees Celsius) to 88 degrees Fahrenheit (31 degrees Celsius). At night the range is 66 degrees Fahrenheit (19 degrees Celsius) to 81 degrees Fahrenheit (27 degrees Celsius).

PLANTS AND ANIMALS

This tropical climate nurtures thousands of plants and animals. The soil and weather of Suriname made it one of the major world producers of sugar in the 1600s. Now, only two sugar plantations exist. Rice is the largest export crop; coffee and cocoa also are grown for sale. Local farmers furnish the Surinamese with a variety of foods, such as citrus fruits and bananas.

More than 150 different kinds of mammals live in the rain

Above: Rice needs lots of water to grow.
Below: Coffee (left) is cultivated on farms, and bananas (right) grow well in the tropical climate.

Some interesting animals in Suriname include
the yagurundi (top), the tapir (left),
and the capybara (above).

A three-toed sloth (left) and an armadillo (above)

forests, including deer and monkeys. The largest, though rarest, mammal is the tapir. Manatees live in the waters of the region. Some of the fiercer animals are the jaguar, the ocelot, and the haka tiger or yagurundi. Other exotic animals include the sloth, the great anteater, the armadillo, and the capybara or bush pig, which is the largest rodent on the planet and, as an adult, looks something like a two-hundred-pound (ninety-kilogram) gerbil. It is reported to be very tasty.

The plant life is extensive and includes many plants whose uses are largely unknown in the developed world. Mark Plotkin, vice president for plant conservation at the Washington-based organization, Conservation International, has gone to Suriname repeatedly to gather medicinal plants from the Trio Indians who

The Trio Indians have helped Mark Plotkin study plants
and their uses. An Indian (left) explains to Plotkin the
medicinal properties of a plant and a shaman (right) holds
a plant he uses in his treatments.

live in the rain forests south of Paramaribo. Because rain-forest
plants have been sources for medicines such as quinine, which
cures malaria, and curare, a powerful drug used to relax muscles
during surgery, Plotkin and others believe that other plants could
be useful for human diseases. The *shamans*, or wise men, of the
Trio tell Plotkin how they use some of the plants. Then Plotkin
gathers samples to take to Washington for research. Tribespeople
use plants to relieve wasp stings, burns, fever, earaches,
snakebites, and other health problems.

In addition to growing many useful plants, Suriname is one of
the keepers of the earth's precious rain forests, which supply
oxygen for all of the earth. This, plus bauxite and rich farmland,
make it a country wealthy in natural resources.

Chapter 2

EXPLORATION AND SETTLEMENT

"DISCOVERY" AND SETTLEMENT

Like other areas of the "New World," Suriname was occupied by native tribes before European exploration began in the late 1400s.

Christopher Columbus was the first European to see the land we now call Suriname, during a voyage in 1498. During the next year, the region was explored by Spaniards. Vicente Yáñez Pinzón was the first European to discover the Amazon River.

Following the "discoveries" of the lush land of Suriname, people from various European countries wanted to come and live in the area. But settlements by the Spanish, British, Dutch, and French all failed until well into the 1600s. Part of the failure was because the native people, who were at first friendly to the newcomers, became hostile when the Europeans tried to enslave them.

In the 1650s a British settlement finally succeeded in Suriname, but it came about in a somewhat unusual way. Barbados, a nearby island in the Caribbean, had sugar plantations that were

A synagogue in Paramaribo

worked by African slaves. There were more slaves than could be put to use. The British governor of the island, Lord Francis Willoughby, sent an expedition to Suriname. When he learned that the land in Suriname could be farmed, he sent experienced plantation owners and many of their slaves to develop new agriculture areas.

In 1662, as a reward for the successful plantations, Charles II of England gave the land to Lord Willoughby and to another English nobleman named Earl Laurens Hide. By 1665 the men had settled in Paramaribo, the present capital.

The settlement attracted other people. Jews came from Portugal and Brazil to escape persecution. They also founded plantations. After learning of the success of the farms, the Dutch began to fight with the British over Suriname as if they were two dogs fighting over a bone. In 1667 a Dutch fleet seized the region. The

This house is built in the Dutch style.

British captured it again quickly, but later that same year, after the Second Anglo-Dutch War, the British gave it to Holland as part of the Treaty of Breda. (Part of what the British received in return was Manhattan Island.)

THE DUTCH INFLUENCE

Except for the years from 1804 to 1816, when Suriname was once again under British rule, the country was under the control of the Netherlands until independence. For hundreds of years, Suriname was known as Dutch Guiana.

One thing Holland did to Suriname, which seems unusual today, was to sell it. The group that bought it included wealthy people who purchased part of it as if they were investing in a company. Another of the owners was the city of Amsterdam and

The Dutch West India Company's headquarters (left) in Amsterdam and the kind of ships the company used to carry their tea and spices (right)

another was the Dutch West India Company, which bought and sold teas and spices around the world.

The dominant activity in Suriname for nearly twenty years was growing sugar. In early times, sugar came only from cane, which grew in the hot, wet climate of the equator. This made it rare and expensive, but those who could afford it were willing to pay for it. The Dutch plantation owners became very wealthy, but their treatment of the slaves who did the actual work grew steadily worse.

The Dutch were successful in Suriname because, in addition to knowing how to build dikes, they brought to the swampy coastal area the knowledge of the polder system of reclaiming land. This is a method of changing the wetland areas, which are at or even below sea level, into useful land. Polder farming involves digging ditches or gullies into the soggy earth and using the excavated earth to raise the level of the land between the ditches. The process is similar to what children do on the beach when they build a sand castle with a moat around it. In poldering, the water stays in the ditches, and the built-up levels have a balance of wet and dry to germinate seeds and grow plants.

Slaves were taken from the west coast of Africa and brought to Suriname.

In modern times, this kind of work is done by large dredging machinery with hydraulic scoops, but in earlier times in Suriname and many other places around the world, the work was done by slaves or poorly paid workers.

SLAVERY

During the 1500s and 1600s, as Europeans founded colonies around the world, they needed labor to work the farms and construct the buildings. The solution lay in kidnapping or buying African slaves. All of the European landowners in Suriname brought African slaves into the country. Members of many different tribes along the western coast of Africa, from Senegal to Angola, were kidnapped and taken across the Atlantic Ocean to Suriname. It is estimated that between 300,000 and 350,000 Africans were imported to Suriname before the practice was made illegal.

A Maroon village

After working to develop the plantations, the slaves were used to grow Suriname's crops. Through the years the slaves rebelled in several ways, including doing their work slowly and, when they could, escaping. It was dangerous to try to escape. If the attempt failed, the slave would be punished severely or even killed. But some succeeded. One of every two hundred slaves is believed to have escaped to live in the dense forests. The escaped slaves were called Maroons. *Maroon* comes from the Spanish word "cimarron," a name used in the Caribbean island of Hispaniola (the island that contains the countries of Haiti and the Dominican Republic) to refer to domestic cattle that had run away to the hills. By the early 1600s the term was used in American colonies as a label for slaves who had successfully escaped from slavery. The former slaves would sneak back to the plantation to steal crops or to visit their loved ones. There were continual battles between these escapees and European soldiers. The Europeans wanted their slaves back and the slaves wanted to stay free.

The details of life in Suriname in the late 1700s are more well known than in many other places in the New World because of one British soldier, John Gabriel Stedman. He joined a corps of eight hundred soldiers sent by the Dutch to help in the fighting between the Europeans who lived in Suriname and the Maroons. By the time Stedman arrived in 1773 to what he called the "Blood Spilling Colony," the land was in chaos. The Europeans were living in gross luxury by exploiting slave labor. The treatment of slaves was some of the worst ever recorded. Their hands and feet were often chopped off for punishment, and some slaves were cruelly tortured and killed.

Slaves had different kinds of duties. There were city slaves and plantation slaves. These groups were divided into slaves for the house, slaves who worked for craftspeople, and slaves who worked in the fields. Sometimes field slaves went to town to work in the house gardens.

Punishments differed, too. Slaves who worked in the house, which was usually far better than working the fields, still were treated very badly. Some were beaten every day simply because the slave owner wished to do so. After working all day in the house, some slaves were required to stay awake all night fanning the whites while they slept. Slaves who worked felling trees were punished more cruelly for trying to escape than others, because escape was easier for those who were already working in the forests.

Stedman kept a journal describing the terrible treatment of the slaves and the "high living" of the Europeans. He also described the plants and animals he saw in the rain forest. A few years after he returned to England, a book based on his diary was published.

William Blake (left) and François-Marie Voltaire (right)

One man who helped produce Stedman's book is famous now. He was William Blake, an Englishman who was an artist and later became a well-known poet. He made his living by preparing art for books. Blake was hired to copy Stedman's watercolors onto metal plates for printing. A famous line from one of Blake's later poems is "Tiger! Tiger! burning bright / In the forests of the night." Perhaps Blake got his idea from Stedman's description, "Tiger-Cat . . . its eyes emitting flashes of lightning" or "Red tiger . . . eyes prominent and sparkling like stars."

Another man who was affected by Stedman's journal was the French writer named François-Marie Voltaire. His most famous book is *Candide.* It is a satire about a man who always says things are for the best—no matter how awful they get. At one point in the book, Candide travels to the New World and meets a slave who has no right hand and no left leg and is wearing only a pair of cotton shorts.

> "Good Heavens!" said Candide to him in Dutch, "What are you doing there, my friend, in this horrible state?"
>
> "I am waiting for my master, the famous merchant Mr. Vanderdendur."

Candide asks about his condition, and the slave says that each of them is given a pair of cotton shorts twice a year for clothes. And, the slave says,

> "When we work in the sugar-mills and the grind-stone catches our fingers, they cut off the hand; when we try to run away, they cut off a leg. Both these things happened to me. This is the price paid for the sugar you eat in Europe. . . . Dogs, monkeys, and parrots are a thousand times less miserable than we are."

Candide weeps and says he may have to give up believing "that everything is well when we are wretched."

The description of the wounded slave was taken from Stedman's book.

Even though Stedman, as a loyal Englishman in the 1700s, was not against slavery, he thought slaves deserved decent treatment. This attitude made him understand why the slaves rebelled.

During this early period, there was no self-government in Suriname. Instead, since it was a colony, the government of the Netherlands was in charge of the country. The laws of the country were the laws that the Netherlands wanted it to have. One of them was that plantation owners could punish slaves as they saw fit. Another law told owners that they had to give slaves food. Each week, slaves who were fourteen years old or older were to be given 9 pounds (4 kilograms) of rice or 8 pounds (3.6 kilograms) of wheat flour or corn flour, or 22 pounds (10 kilograms) of yams, or a few other foodstuffs. Those younger than fourteen received half the allotment.

Colonial administrators ran the country from day to day. They were chosen from the most successful plantation owners. A few of them received the title of colonial governor.

An area of Paramaribo near the harbor

GROWTH OF PARAMARIBO

As the plantations brought wealth to the country, the city of Paramaribo grew. Before the late 1700s, in Suriname as in most other parts of the world, most people lived in the country instead of in cities. But the need for clergymen, wood and metal workers, traders, civil servants (men who worked for the growing colonial government), and soldiers who captured runaway slaves drew more and more people to Paramaribo. It was and still is Suriname's largest city.

A European slave merchant bargains to purchase an African chief's prisoners of war.

In 1791, 9,650 people lived in Paramaribo, about one-fifth of the country's counted population of 49,000. Suriname's population at that time was mostly slaves. Only 3,360 of the 49,000 people were white, and nearly all of them lived in the cities. The other 45,640 were slaves. The people living in the forests were not counted.

SLAVERY BECOMES ILLEGAL

The whites came from many ethnic groups: Dutch, Jewish, British, French, and German. The Dutch, of course, were mostly in charge. Some of the French came for religious reasons, as did the Moravians from Germany, who came as missionaries and began the large Protestant community that continues today. The vast imbalance between Europeans and Africans began to change when slavery was finally made illegal. The selling of slaves was outlawed in 1814 in all Dutch territories. However, many Africans were still smuggled into the country.

Chicago Southwest Christian School
OAK LAWN BUILDING
10110 SOUTH CENTRAL AVENUE
Oak Lawn, Illinois 60453

Even though slaves could no longer be brought into the country legally, the practice of slavery was not abolished in Suriname until 1863. By that time, there were thirty-three thousand slaves. This small number—only one-tenth of the total brought to the country—is a result of the terrible treatment slaves received and of the fact that many more men than women were brought as slaves. These things kept the population from growing.

When the government outlawed slavery it said that, although the thirty-three thousand were no longer slaves, they had to work for ten more years as laborers with contracts under which they would be paid. The slaves understood their new freedom in different ways. It meant an end to the flogging, the iron chains, and to other devices used to punish slaves. It also meant an end to the harsh labor in the fields. But some of the slaves thought they might be able to live like their wealthy masters. Former slaves took holidays when they wanted—some lasting for weeks or even months. Many of them could not be lured back even by promises of fewer hours or of raised wages. The fact was that the master-slave relationship had destroyed any kind of goodwill that might have existed between owners and workers. The workforce declined dramatically. Meanwhile, many African Americans simply set up their own villages, divided farmland among themselves, and created their own independent lives.

NEW PLANTATION WORKERS

The loss of slaves was a big problem for plantation owners. There were no machines to do the work, so other workers were sought, and many were brought from China. Some came under

Chinese-owned businesses in the capital today

five-year contracts. After the term was up, many chose to return to China. Those who stayed behind began their own farms or started other businesses.

What this meant for the Dutch landowners was that it became more and more difficult to find people who would do the hard labor on the plantations. Another source of workers had to be found. That source was India, a British colony. Between 1873, a decade after the slaves were freed, and 1916, about thirty-four thousand East Indians were brought to Suriname. They too came under contracts, which meant they agreed to work a certain number of years. Most (82 percent) were Hindus who practiced

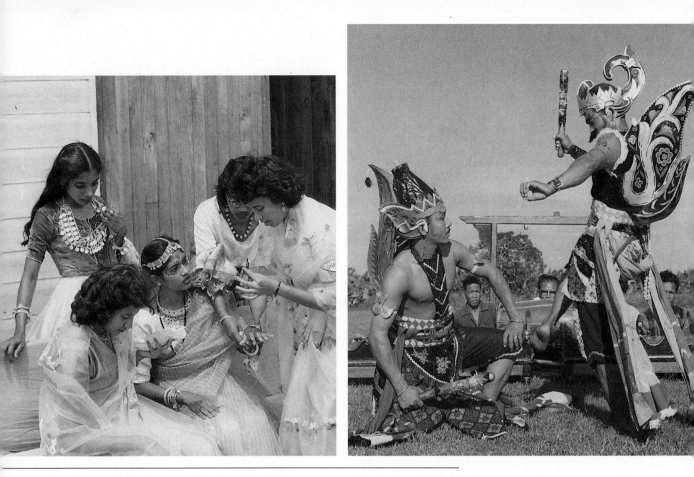

Left: Hindustani bridesmaids help prepare a bride for her wedding.
Right: Indonesians perform a traditional dance.

the religion of Hinduism. The rest were Muslims, followers of Islam. About one-third of them left the country after their contracts expired. The East Indians who settled are referred to as Hindustanis.

The last group of imported workers came from another Dutch colony, the Nederlands-India (Netherlands, or Dutch, East Indies), which is now Indonesia. They came from the island of Java and are called Javanese. From 1890 until 1939, more than thirty-three thousand Indonesians came to Suriname to work the plantations. By 1947 more than eight thousand had returned to their native country.

Suriname is a pluralistic society with people from many ethnic, racial, and religious backgrounds.

Because of the plantation economy and the importation of slaves and contract workers, plus the arrival of missionaries and other Europeans seeking easier or better lives, Suriname became a pluralistic society, a society with people from many ethnic, racial, and religious backgrounds who have different customs and often speak different languages. For a long time Suriname was known for the peaceful coexistence of different ethnic groups, but that reputation is changing. Friction and violence have grown, partly because of government and military actions.

Suriname's rivers were important to its development, and are still vital factors in the lives of the people.

Chapter 3

SURINAME WORKS TOWARD INDEPENDENCE

Suriname went through several forms of government as it moved from the status of a colony to that of an independent nation. The process began after slavery was abolished in 1863. The first change came from the Dutch and was imposed on January 1, 1866. The plan was called the Surinamese Government Order.

THE DUTCH KEEP CONTROL

A representative body of thirteen people was formed by the Netherlands to make domestic decisions affecting Suriname. This group was allowed to make decisions about local matters, but the king in the Netherlands kept most of the power. For instance, budgets had to be approved by the king, and he could declare rules illegal if he wished. Of the thirteen members, four were selected by the governor of the country, who was selected by the king; the other nine were elected by people in Suriname. However, the only people who could vote were those who paid a certain amount of taxes, which meant voters had to be well off. This law kept poor people, including most of the people who had been slaves or contract laborers, from voting.

Creole women

Over the next fifty years, the powers of this small legislative body shrank because the Dutch feared that the men in Suriname wanted to become independent of their "mother country," and the Netherlands government wanted to remain in charge.

While the established government in Paramaribo was trying to work with the powers in the Netherlands, other racial groups within Suriname wanted to be recognized by the government and to participate in its decisions. Also, many people in these groups wanted to be able to earn more money, and they felt that those in power stifled their abilities to do so. After 1900 the power of the white population (fewer than two people of every one hundred were white) began to decline, and other groups, such as the Creoles and Hindustanis, gained more power. *Creoles* are people of mixed African and European descent.

An event outside the country had a widespread effect in the 1930s. The Great Depression, caused by a collapse of financial markets, began in the United States and spread through many countries of the world. Depressions make trade slow down or even stop for some goods. Because countries rely on trade to move goods into and out of the country and to maintain their wealth, this "slowdown" means that products cannot be sold and do not need to be manufactured. Companies close and workers are laid off. In Suriname, as in other countries, there was unemployment and poverty during the Great Depression. The government did little to help the common people. Instead it prevented unions from forming because it was afraid of the power of mass movements.

STIRRINGS OF INDEPENDENCE

One outspoken leader of the people was Anton de Kom. (Later he wrote a book about slavery in Suriname.) De Kom, a Creole, wanted people to put aside their ethnic differences and become simply Surinamese. He thought this would help unite the nation and stop the wasting of human potential. The government reacted to his anger by ousting him from the country.

In the 1940s after the Great Depression, things began to change in Suriname. The country's wealth grew, and some citizens of Suriname began to agitate for Suriname to become an independent country. Meanwhile Queen Wilhelmina of the Netherlands also wanted changes made in the ways that her country was connected to Suriname. She began making reforms in 1945. The changes happened without violence, but there were problems. A large question was how power would transfer from the Netherlands to Suriname. Who would hold the power in the newly independent country?

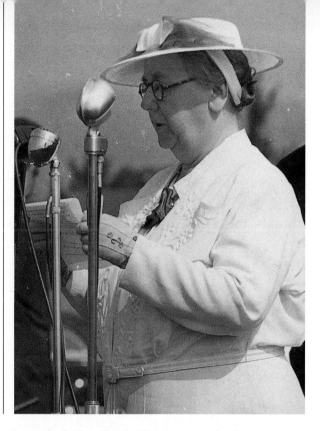

Queen Wilhelmina of the Netherlands, photographed in 1942

Because the Dutch had settled the land, Europeans had always had the most powerful positions. But other groups wanted that to change. As more and more Creoles began to work for the government, they made gains in both wealth and power. They had good reason to expect that they could continue to gain, and it seemed to them that they were the next logical group to run the country once the Europeans had given up power. The Javanese and the Hindustanis also wanted universal suffrage—the right of all adults to vote. The Dutch finally agreed with that arrangement and universal suffrage became law.

Political parties were formed. The Suriname Progressive People's Party (PVS) was composed of less-well-off Creoles. It also was favored by members of the Roman Catholic Church. The party favored universal suffrage but it was not a dominant party for very long. By contrast, three other parties have had strong roles in Suriname's political life. The National Partij Suriname

(NPS) arose in reaction to the idea of universal suffrage and was peopled primarily by Creoles who had worked their way into positions of power and wanted to continue as leaders in the country. The United Hindu Party (VHP) did not want the Creoles to maintain so much power. Finally, the Indonesian Joint Peasants' Party (KTPI) served to unite the descendants of people who had come to Suriname from Indonesia.

These ethnic divisions and loyalties pushed social issues to the background. The result was that corruption grew as leaders chose to help their friends rather than try to make changes in the country.

Suriname held its first full election in 1948. Many representatives from the Javanese, the Hindustanis, and the Creoles were elected. This ended the Creoles' grasp for power. Over the next decade the Creoles became merely another one of Suriname's interest groups.

In 1954 there was a shift in the political status of the country. The Netherlands voted to change the country's status from colonial to territorial. The Netherlands maintained a strong tie to the country, which was still known as Dutch Guiana, but the relationship was looser than it had been. Suriname citizens had more control. Some were unhappy about the change, and many Surinamese decided to move to the Netherlands.

Meanwhile, with splintered interests often overriding what was good for the whole country, some of the Surinamese who had moved to the Netherlands, especially college students, were gaining new understandings. They were learning about their country's situation by studying other countries that had been freed of colonial rule. They also were conscious of a new and

A statue of Queen Wilhelmina in Paramaribo represented what the Surinamese did not want to be.

surprising attitude from the Dutch toward them, a negative attitude. Even though the Surinamese spoke good Dutch and knew about Dutch culture from the Suriname schools, the Dutch people in the Netherlands treated the Surinamese like foreigners and expected them to have their own culture. This treatment made the students want Suriname to be totally free and independent of the Netherlands.

Eventually the pressures of the pro-Suriname people led to the formation in 1961 of a new political party, the Nationalist Republican Party (PNR), the first one devoted to making the country independent. This party also wanted a smaller gap between the rich and the poor, they wanted foreign investors out of the country, and they wanted the country to see itself as one nation.

A poem written by Surinamese poet Robin Raveles called "Wan Bon" or "One Tree" captures this idea:

One tree
So many leaves
One tree

One river
So many creeks
All flow to one sea

One head
So many thoughts
Thoughts including one good one

One god
So many ways to worship him
But one Father

One Suriname
So many kinds of hair
So many colors of skin
So many languages
One people

Published with the consent of the government of Suriname through the Director of the Department of Cultural Affairs.

This poem has become an unofficial national song for the country.

But the numerous political parties traded power from election to election. While the PNR received a good deal of publicity, it never gained actual elected power within the government.

*Henck Arron, center, stands proudly as Suriname's flag
is raised as a new member of the United Nations.*

However, in 1973 a Creole named Henck Arron was elected prime minister. The following year he announced his intention to make Suriname an independent nation. Another leader, East Indian Jaggernath Lachmon, worked with Arron and other leaders to prepare for independence. They were concerned about racial balance in the armed forces and human rights guarantees in the constitution.

INDEPENDENCE

Many people were uneasy about what would happen to the control of the country when the Netherlands was no longer a powerful force in Suriname. But the new constitution was

The Parliament Building in Paramaribo

approved, and the peaceful change took place November 25, 1975. Suriname's newly independent country was to be run by a parliamentary system of government that has one house, the National Assembly.

Despite the enthusiasm of some for this new status, the leaders, Arron, Lachmon, Johan Ferrier (the republic's first president) and others, unfortunately could not heal the ethnic frictions that had been rising. The disagreements about how to change the economy, what to do with foreign investors, and if and how banking and insurance should be changed remained areas of disagreement. This lack of direction took a toll on the population. Nearly one-third of Suriname's citizens, about 150,000 people—many educated and well off—emigrated to the Netherlands over the next few years. Meanwhile, Suriname remained strongly dependent on the Dutch for economic assistance.

Desi Bouterse

A mere five years into Suriname's independence, everything changed. A violent military coup on February 25, 1980, yanked the elected government from power. After the leaders were removed by force, a military sergeant named Desi Bouterse rose to power. Bouterse installed an eight-man military council called the Nationale Militaire Raad (NMR) to take charge. President Ferrier objected and appointed a civilian group led by Dr. Henk Chin A. Sen, who was a former leader of the PNR. In August Bouterse staged a coup and replaced President Ferrier with Chin A. Sen. The legislature was dissolved and a state of emergency was declared. The Hindustanis inspired a coup against Bouterse that failed. Bouterse formed a political alliance called the Revolutionary People's Front, which included leaders of the NMR and leaders from workers' and student groups.

In February 1982 the NMR, led by Bouterse, seized power from

Bouterse's men even brought weapons to a news conference.

Dr. Chin A. Sen and the civilian government. I. Fred Ramdat
Misier was named interim president. To try to keep aid coming
from the Netherlands, a twelve-member Cabinet with a civilian
majority was appointed by Bouterse's government, and a
moderate economist named Henry Neyjorst became prime
minister. Nevertheless, business groups, left-wing groups, and
trade unions all spoke out against the lack of social and economic
management by the government. They called for a return to
constitutional rule.

Bouterse's government responded by imposing more censorship
and arresting a prominent trade union leader named Cyriel Daal.
This prompted strikes and demonstrations, and Bouterse promised
an election in March 1983. But in December 1982 the government
increased the violence of its suppression. Military leaders, directed
by Bouterse, threw firebombs into radio stations, a newspaper

office, and union headquarters. Fourteen prominent men who were university professors, lawyers, leading journalists, and leaders in the trade unions were arrested. The military tortured and killed these men, including Daal.

This show of force caused outcries from many nations. It was clear that Bouterse had little intention of running the country as a democracy. Both the United States and the Netherlands cut off the financial aid they had given Suriname, which caused the country even more problems.

The government continued to shift and remained unstable until late in 1985, when a new constitution was written that would return the country to civilian rule. During this process, former prime minister Henck Arron of the NPS, Jaggernath Lachmon of the Hindustani-based VHP, and Willy Soemita of the KTPI accepted offers to join the dominant NMR, which had been named the Supreme Council.

The constitution was approved in September 1987 by 93 percent of the voters, even though there were concerns about the distribution of power. Meanwhile, in the intervening years, lack of aid from the Netherlands added even more strain to Suriname's suffering economy. The general election for the 51-seat National Assembly, held in November 1987, resulted in a strong win—40 seats—for the Front for Democracy and Development (FDO), a party that was forged from an alliance of the NPS, VHP, and KTPI. Ramsewak Shankar became president and Arron became vice-president. Bouterse was named leader of a five-member military council and many believed, that despite the appearance of a civilian government, Bouterse continued to exercise a great deal of power.

Ronnie Brunswijk, center, led the Jungle Commando.

Bouterse's rule was not easily accepted by all citizens. There were several violent encounters between the official military and a group of Maroons. The Maroons' leader is a man named Ronnie Brunswijk, who was originally part of the coup when Bouterse took over. He had been a bodyguard for Bouterse. He was fired and not given his pay. This angered him, and after trying to make a living in low-paying jobs, he organized a rebellion against Bouterse's soldiers. Brunswijk's group was named the Jungle Commando.

The rebels did not have enough power or enough people to succeed in their subsequent efforts to take over a military post, a garrison, and an arsenal. But soldiers were killed, and the government took the rebellion seriously. They fought back by harassing Maroons, arresting them, and ultimately killing more than a hundred Maroon men, women, and children during raids

The headquarters of the Jungle Commando

on villages. The murders inspired more battles, and others joined the Jungle Commando. Meanwhile, some Maroons experienced new opportunities and prosperity under Bouterse's rule. They did not want to have anything to do with the Jungle Commando.

In addition to the Maroons' difficulties, objections were raised by other native groups about the insensitive treatment of minorities and the blending of ethnic groups into a unified identity of nationalism was not successful. Friction continued among the ethnic-centered political parties. The Hindustanis, who had become a large segment of the population, grew in economic power.

Despite the strivings for a democratic government, the violence and disputes did not end. Elections were held and Ramsewak Shankar became president, but the military continued to exercise force. On Christmas Eve in 1990, the head of the military took

Commander Ivan Graanoogst

over, displacing the three-year-old civilian government of President Shankar. There were no murders, but such actions showed that the government was unstable. The new military leader was Commander Ivan Graanoogst, but the belief was that the real power continued to be held by Desi Bouterse.

Bouterse's power was shown when the interim president, Johan Kraag, invited Bouterse to return to command the armed forces. An election was held in May 1991, and the FDO won thirty of the fifty-one seats, so the old leadership of the country continued to dominate the government.

Since independence from the Netherlands, Suriname's government has had more failures than successes in taking care of social and economic problems in the country. Many of Suriname's brightest citizens have emigrated, and dissatisfaction among various ethnic groups is growing. The challenges facing Suriname are large and its future is unpredictable.

Chapter 4

CULTURE AND SOCIETY

ETHNIC DIVERSITY

Ethnic groups from four continents live in Suriname. Many of their ancestors arrived as slaves or as indentured servants. The country has perhaps the greatest ethnic diversity of any country in the "New World," which is remarkable, considering its relatively small size.

To explore Suriname's culture and society, one needs to understand the many ethnic groups that live in the small country of Suriname and how they have done so for centuries in relative peace, at least for most of that time.

The main groups in Suriname—in the order in which they came to the country—are the Amerindians, the Dutch, the British, the Africans, the Portuguese, the Chinese, the Hindustanis, and the Indonesians (Javanese). The same list can be arranged in other ways. One would be by how many there are of each group now, in addition to groups native to the country. To do this, another group must be added, the Creoles. A list of the groups from largest to smallest population looks like this: Hindustanis, 38 percent; Creoles, 30 percent; Javanese, 15 percent; Maroons, 10 percent (of which 10,000 are refugees in French Guiana); Amerindians, 3 percent; Chinese, 2 percent; Europeans, Lebanese, and others, 1 percent.

Opposite page: A Javanese woman buys eggplants from a Hindustani vendor.

Yet another list can be arranged by power. This power is in economics and government, so the groups nearest to the top earn the most money and are now, or have been, the most involved in making decisions about the country. This list is not as clear-cut as others, but some things are obvious. The Europeans had almost all the power and money for centuries. In the past several decades, some of this power as well as some of the money has shifted to the Creoles and the Hindustanis.

LANGUAGE

A few of the more important features of a culture are language, religion, and education. When Suriname was settled by people from several parts of the world, a key "import" was language. As early as 1700, a new language had been developed by the slaves so they could talk with each other. It was a combination of the West African languages from their home tribes and countries with English, Dutch, and Portuguese, the languages of the rulers and the slave traders. The language is called Sranan Tongo. It is now spoken by most Suriname citizens, but that was not always the case. For a long time, the Dutch and other people in power called the language "Taki-Taki." They tried to ignore it and pretend that it was not important.

The official language of the country, of course, is Dutch because the Dutch ruled the country for such a long time. If people wanted to gain status and power, they learned to speak Dutch and learned about Dutch culture.

But because of the many ethnic groups that settled Suriname, many languages still are spoken there. There are five Amerindian languages in the country. Arawak and Carib, which are the names of original tribes, are spoken along the coast. The other three are spoken by people who live in the forests. These are Trio, Wajana, and Akoerio, which are tribal as well as language names.

The Maroons, who have African ancestry, speak languages from two main families. One includes the Saramaccan, Matawai, and Kwinti, which are spoken by Creoles in western Suriname. The other is made up of Ndjuka, Paramacan, and Aluku, which are spoken in the east.

Sarnami Hindustani is the name of the Hindi dialect spoken in Suriname. Hindi is one of the main languages in India; it was brought to Suriname with the contract laborers.

The Javanese language, brought by the Indonesians to Suriname, has undergone some changes, as is often the case when speakers are separated by a great distance for a long time. Both Dutch and Sranan Tongo words are part of the revised language, which is called Javanese.

A closer look at the Javanese language illustrates some of the differences in cultures that are revealed in language. Javanese uses sixteen different styles of speech, depending on the relationship of the speaker to the listener. If the listener is older and a friend, there is one style; if the listener is older and a stranger, there is another. There are different styles for speaking to younger people, too. There also are five different levels of politeness that are attached to words. For instance, the word "I" is *aku* when speaking to a younger brother or sister, but when speaking to parents or grandparents, the speaker refers to himself or herself as *kula*. There are nearly a thousand words that change like this. By the time children have grown to their teen years, they are expected to know most of this complex system.

While Javanese people enjoy boisterous conversations, silence is also important in their language. In many cultures, silence is a form of rudeness, but Javanese visitors and hosts sometimes have long silences during a visit and no one feels uncomfortable.

Not all Creoles speak languages derived from Africa. Some, who are rich and of a high status, speak the Surinamese version of Dutch as their native language. It is called Surinaams-Nederlands and has undergone changes since the Dutch colonized the land more than three hundred years ago.

There are small numbers of people who speak a dialect of Chinese or Arabic. The Jewish communities have grown so small that German and Portuguese are no longer spoken as a first language.

Many Surinamese speak Sranan Tongo, Dutch, English, and the language of their ethnic group.

Finally, it is important to note that the mixing of people and cultures in such a small area has meant that parts of languages have crossed from one people to another. Examples of a few words that come from the native Amerindians—the Arawak and Carib tribes—are *barbecue, canoe, cannibal,* and *iguana.*

THE ABSENCE OF SPANISH

A particularly important part of Surinamese culture, which relates to language, derives from the history of the area. Unlike most of the countries in South America and many of the islands in the Caribbean Sea between South and North America, Suriname was not settled by the Spanish. The power and influence of the Dutch in Suriname (and of the French in Suriname's neighboring country to the east, French Guiana) was held by the Spanish in most other countries. In the past several

Basket weaving is one of the many artistic reflections of Surinamese culture.

years, this difference has been seen as a handicap. Both the trading of goods and the sharing of culture would be simpler if Suriname had Spanish as its national language. Such a move would be complicated and difficult. Meanwhile, Spanish is taught in schools and is being employed more and more in business.

LITERATURE AND THE ARTS

The broad range of ethnic groups living in Suriname means that there are many artistic reflections of culture—pottery, clothing, poetry, music, wood carving, calabash carving, dance, music, and storytelling.

Poetry is important and popular in Suriname. Two of the country's best poets are Michael Slory and Shrini Vasi. Slory writes in Dutch as well as in Sranan Tongo, and he has won many prizes. Another of their great writers is Ismene Krishnadadh, who writes for children ages eight to twelve. In 1993 she won Suriname's national literary prize, which is awarded every other year. Another rising writer is Marta Tjoe Nie, who writes both novels and poems.

Painter Nola Hatterman, who moved to Suriname from Holland, died in the early 1980s. She is honored as a great painter. The Painters' Institute is named after her and the artists whom she trained are the leading painters in the country.

One famous art form of Suriname comes from the Maroons. The Maroons, like many other people around the world, use art to express love or unhappiness or as a way to celebrate with one another. The men have carving tools, such as knives, chisels, and compasses, to carve wood or the thick skin of the gourdlike calabash fruit, which is used for scoops and containers of food. Women also carve the calabashes, but they use pieces of broken glass for tools. The men carve designs that they saw when they spent time in the cities—straight lines and perfect curves. The women carve the organic and uneven shapes they are familiar with in the forests. The Maroons give away their work as gifts of love.

Another way the Maroons express themselves is through music. Popular songs, called *seketi*, are composed by nearly everyone. They may compose while paddling a canoe or preparing food. Children are embraced and encouraged to create little tunes out of their thoughts. When people gather to sing and dance, the songs

Above: A Maroon mother and child walk past a wooden house decorated with a carved design.
Below: Some young musicians

*Saramaccan women wear skirts that are simple rectangles
with different patterns and stripes.*

are sung with many repetitions as friends clap and dance. Some
songs are popular for a while, but most of them disappear as new
ones are composed. Songs often have to do with love or hate,
anger or joy. Sometimes the songs concern the business of
everyone. For instance, when the giant Afobaka hydroelectric dam
was built in the 1960s and thousands of people had to move
away from their villages, many people composed songs of anger.

But many seketi are personal. A man who was going away to
work expressed his fear of being knifed by a fellow laborer from
Colombia in this song:

I'm calling out for help, everyone,

I'm calling out for help against them.

I'm calling out for help against the "Amigos" [Colombians].

A cultural expression of the Saramaccan tribe is the naming of
fabric patterns. The Saramaccan women have skirts that are
simple rectangles with different patterns and stripes. Rather than
referring to them by style, color, or arrangement of fabric, they

Javanese women like to wear brightly colored clothing.

name the item by an event that occurred when the skirt was sewed. Some of the names are inspired by events, such as *Amerika go a gadu,* "the first American astronauts landed on the moon"; *Agbago waka a opolani,* when Chief Agbago took his first plane ride to Paramaribo; or *Wata booko Milanda,* to commemorate a 1949 flood that ruined a Paramaribo store patronized by Maroons. Sometimes humorous events or scandals inspire names, too. A woman's skirts are a way of tracking history, both her own and that of her village and the culture.

Women's clothing is an artful expression for the Suriname-Javanese, too. The women dress in batik fabric. A wax design or picture is painted onto cloth and then the cloth is dyed. Wherever there is wax, the dye cannot penetrate. The women use this fabric to make fancy turbans that they wrap around their heads and sarongs, dresses that wrap around the body. Maroon women wear kerchiefs on their heads and long calico dresses.

Other elements of culture that give us information about life in a country are religion and education. These are both important because they show what people value.

RELIGION

Many religious groups thrive in Suriname, including Hindus, Roman Catholics, Protestants, Muslims (followers of Islam), and Jews. Most religions came with the people who migrated here. Other religions were brought by missionaries or developed by Surinamese who did not want to practice the religions of their parents.

The Amerindian religion centers on *animism*, a belief in many kinds of spirits. A shaman communicates with the spirits to help guide the lives of the believers.

The Creoles have two religions. One is Roman Catholicism and the other is Winti. When missionaries came in the 1700s, they converted many African slaves to Christianity. Today, many Creoles attend Catholic churches and schools. The second religion, Winti, has many spirits and ghosts that participate in people's daily lives. Part of Winti comes from African religions. As part of the religion, special members go into trances—often during long outdoor ceremonies that include dances and walking on hot coals without burning their feet.

Closely related to African religions is the religion practiced by the Maroons. Ritual life is the centerpiece of Maroon communities. Members are bound together through ceremonies for handling life's difficulties, ceremonies to receive messages from spirits, and ceremonies related to shrines.

St. Peter and Paul Cathedral, said to be the largest completely wooden cathedral in South America, was recently restored.

Imported religion played an interesting role in the life of slavery. Slave owners did not want clergy preaching the Christian doctrine of equality and compassion for social outcasts and oppressed people because they feared it would inspire the slaves to revolt. They also feared that the slaves might demand to have Sundays free of work and expect to celebrate Christian holidays, too. Nevertheless, missionaries came. Spanish and Portuguese Jesuit missionaries tried to convert the Indians and the Maroons.

In 1735 the Moravian Brethren began their preaching among the Maroons, and thirty years later they began work in Paramaribo. Their numbers grew and today it is one of the largest Christian denominations in the country. The other is Roman Catholic. The Catholics began their work with the slaves in 1787. Other churches, such as the Lutheran and the Dutch Reformed, did not work to convert the masses but instead remained the churches of the slave masters.

An Islamic mosque in the center of Paramaribo

Other Christian churches that have sent missionaries to gain converts include Methodist, African Methodist Episcopal, Baptist, Seventh-Day Adventist, Jehovah's Witness, and Pentecostal. Membership in these churches totals about twenty-two thousand. The Roman Catholics have eighty thousand members.

Because of the horrors of the Spanish Inquisition in the 1600s, when Jews and others were tortured and put to death, many Jews came to Suriname. So many came that they referred to themselves as a "Hebrew nation" and built two temples. But today the Jewish population is small.

Islam is practiced by all Suriname-Javanese (or Indonesians) and some East Indians. Because of their different roots, the people follow slightly different forms. Muslims believe in a just, loving, and merciful God, and they do not separate faith from works.

A Hindu shrine on the outskirts of Paramaribo

Ritual feasts are an important part of the religion as well as pleasing the spirits.

Most of the East Indians follow Hinduism, which has a variety of practices, too. One of the focuses is on spirits, while other Hindustanis focus on ideas. The goal of Hinduism is to escape the cycle of rebirth and the suffering brought on by one's own actions.

CULTURAL DIVERSITY

The people who settled in Suriname brought their own histories along with their own religions, languages, and lifestyles. Even though many ethnic groups in Suriname have been here for hundreds of years, they have kept their cultural heritage alive. These groups create a rich and varied cultural life for Suriname.

These Amerindians live in Albina.

Chapter 5

A CLOSER LOOK
AT THE SURINAMESE

While a few citizens of Suriname are recent immigrants, almost all Surinamese are from families that have lived in the country for two, three, or more generations. They all call themselves Surinamese, but their backgrounds shape their individual lives in many different ways. Their religions, the kinds of work they do, and the daily customs they practice have grown out of the histories of each group's origins and from their earliest days.

AMERINDIANS

Most of the Amerindians, members of the Arawak and Carib tribes, have stayed in the forested interior of the country where they first hid to keep from becoming enslaved by the Europeans.

Before Europeans arrived, these Amerindian tribes and others spread throughout the chain of islands that bridges the Caribbean Sea from Venezuela to Florida. The Caribs were a warring tribe and had driven the Arawak off the islands. This was true, also, for the tribe called Surinen, which gave its name to the area but is now extinct.

Archaeologists say long before the Europeans arrived, from

Amerindians live along the Marowijne River (left).
Medicine made from plants will help cure this boy's earache (right).

about 2000 B.C., the Arawak were planting and harvesting
vegetables and living in villages with one large hut for meetings
and ceremonies.

Life for them depended on understanding how nature works.
For instance, leaf-cutting ants can strip a tree in a single night and
they also like the leaves of plants that people cultivate, including
corn. Immigrants tried to outwit the ants for centuries by using
smoke, poison, and explosives. Nothing worked, so they finally
decided to follow the customs of the Amerindians. When ants
move in, people move out. It usually takes the ants a few years of
random foraging before they locate the new field that the
Amerindians planted. When they do, the people move on.

Despite hundreds of years of isolation from Suriname's urban
areas, in the late 1980s, the tribal people succeeded in having a
representative elected to the National Assembly.

The bush *is the forested area where the Maroons live.*

MAROONS

The Maroons are the only African slaves in the New World who succeeded in escaping their captors and rebuilding a full tribal, traditional life such as they once had in Africa. Sometimes called Bush Negroes, the Maroons live in the forested area called the bush. They farm for themselves and earn a living by fishing and trading, both with other Maroons and with Amerindians. These groups have made their homes in the districts of Marowijne, Brokopondo, and Nickerie.

A Saramaccan woman carrying skirt cloth on her head

Their way of life has been threatened often. When they first escaped in the 1600s and 1700s, they battled continually against the plantation owners and the soldiers to keep their freedom. From 1760 to 1770, peace treaties were signed with three major Maroon groups, the Saramacca, Ndjuka, and the Paramaka. One of the slave leaders from the time, Kwaku, is honored with a statue in Paramaribo.

The Saramacca and the Ndjuka are the largest groups, together totaling about fifty thousand people; the Paramaka have about four thousand people. The peace between the Maroons and the government held steady for about two centuries, but in the 1980s disputes arose. One of the causes of frustration on the part of the Maroons was the building of the Afobaka Dam in the mid-1960s. In the Brokopondo Valley of the Suriname River, there were forty-three villages where six thousand people lived. These people, from the Saramacca tribe, and their ancestors had lived along the river

A member of the Jungle Commando

for three hundred years. They used the river for transportation, washing, drinking, fishing, sport, and to carry away sewage. The construction of the dam gave many of the Maroons a chance to earn money for a while, but the huge lake that formed behind the dam flooded the forty-three villages. The company moved the people to other locations, but life changed for them in ways they never would have chosen. The people had no say in the matter, because Suriname needed to sell its bauxite.

Disagreements and battles, though not constant, are still taking place between the Maroons' fighters—the Jungle Commando—and the National Army of Suriname.

Even though Maroons have contact with urban life in Suriname, many of their traditional ways of life continue. Many Saramaccan men go to the coast for months or years at a time to find jobs and earn money.

Meanwhile the wives and children who are left behind continue

Saramaccan men dressed in their finest to attend a funeral

the work of the villages. The women have rice gardens—they can choose from more than seventy varieties of rice—and they grow manioc, okra, yams, and other vegetables. They embroider capes, neckerchiefs, and sew other decorative or useful gifts for their husbands. The stitching the women do for their husbands is done with artfulness and care, while the skirts and other things they sew for themselves are put together quickly. The husbands, in turn, carve beautiful wooden trays, combs, and other objects for their wives.

Men and women are important in different ways among the Maroons. The women are important because the family line is carried through them. When a baby girl is born, there is a special celebration because the family line will continue. Men are important because they are the ones who go away to earn money for needed things such as kerosene, soap, and salt. Girls usually have one trip to the city to see what it is like.

Some Maroon men leave village life and move to the coast for good. This has meant that more women than men live in the villages. This is one reason why a Maroon man has more than one wife. Divorce, too, is quite common, either by a man who does not think his wife is carrying out her responsibilities or by a woman who cannot get pregnant.

Mothers and children are close for the first several years of a child's life. They sleep together and spend almost all their days together. When the children are a little older, six or seven, they might spend time with other relatives if the mother needs to spend a day harvesting rice. An older child may live with other nearby relatives to help them with chores or to give the mother time to take care of a new baby.

Because these people have lived in the rain forests for so long, they know many things about the plants and animals there. These villagers, especially the older ones, have helped scientists from other parts of the world who are looking for medicinal plants in the rain forests.

This may change, though. In recent years, more and more young people, both men and women, are choosing to move to Paramaribo or other cities. They want city jobs so they can earn money to buy things. They no longer want to do the kinds of work done by their older relatives.

Of course, supplies of some of the resources have shrunk, too. In some areas there are fewer wild animals and far fewer fish because of industry. But mostly, young people just want to become part of city life. Many of the older people are sad to see the knowledge of life in the forests disappear.

Some Creole women wear traditional clothing (above), while others mix traditional and contemporary clothes (right).

CREOLES

The Africans who moved to the cities after the emancipation have spent generations becoming more like the Dutch. Many of them married Europeans and had families. This group became larger and larger until they gained their own identity and name: the Creoles. Many of them joined the churches of the European missionaries. They learned to speak and write Dutch and became educated in the Dutch culture. Some Creoles worked either as farmers in Coronie and Para or for industries in Para or Marowijne. Others, who spoke Dutch and adopted the cultural ways of the Dutch, became government workers in Paramaribo. Their knowledge and adopted culture helped them gain power, and many of them now have important positions in the government.

Javanese women in the market

JAVANESE

Another segment of Suriname citizens is made up of the Javanese. They, too, came to Suriname from a distant continent—from the island country of Indonesia, off the southeastern part of mainland Asia.

Thousands of Javanese came in the early 1900s to work as contract laborers. About eight thousand returned to their homeland, but more than thirty thousand stayed on to live in Suriname.

In current times, some of the Javanese, or Suriname-Javanese as they also are called, live in small villages and farm in the district of Commewijne, while others live in the cities. Many Javanese in Paramaribo work for the government; Javanese hold the top positions in the department of agriculture. One of the radio stations broadcasts in the Javanese language.

HINDUSTANIS

The Hindustanis, whose ancestors were brought from India for contract labor work, dominate the population now. They make up more than one-third of the population of Suriname.

These British Indian subjects who came to Suriname held unusual positions as contract workers, because they remained British subjects and could appeal to the British consul. However, life in the fields did not make such appeals an easy solution to problems.

Like other such workers, the Hindustanis were expected to work seven hours a day in the factory or ten hours a day in the fields, five days a week. The bosses often used racial insults to try to get the people to work harder, but it made the people angry. There were some violent strikes that occurred when wages were reduced and workers were not allowed to talk with authorities. It was not until 1930 that Suriname and the Netherlands decided against contract immigration.

Now more Hindustanis than any other ethnic group work for the government. Many still farm in the districts of Nickerie, Saramacca, and Suriname. In the cities, Hindustanis hold professional positions such as doctors and lawyers.

EUROPEANS

Many descendants of Europeans have returned to Europe. Their ancestors were usually the plantation owners or professionals, or they may have had powerful positions in the government. Those still in Suriname live mostly in and around Paramaribo, as they have for hundreds of years.

Surinamese markets are a multi-cultural experience.
A Dutch woman (left) looks at fabric and an Indian woman
checks the produce a Chinese man is selling (right).

The exception is the whites who live as missionaries. They live in small towns and villages as well as in the cities.

CHINESE

The Chinese also came to Suriname as contract laborers. Of those who have stayed, many have carried on with traditional farming, as their ancestors did. The difference, though, is that now the farmers own their own land and negotiate for fair prices. Others live in the cities where they run small businesses.

IDENTITY

All Surinamese carry another identity and another history, except for the Amerindians. For everyone else—Maroons, Creoles, Javanese, Hindustanis, Europeans, and Chinese—personal history reaches across one ocean or another to distant lands. How does this affect Suriname?

Above: The roof of this house on stilts has air vents to let hot air escape.
Below: Women stroll past a fountain in the center of Paramaribo.

Chapter 6

LIVING IN SURINAME

City life in Suriname blends customs from the ethnic groups that occupy the country with the demands of living in a tropical weather zone.

Many buildings have roofs that rise steeply in the custom of Dutch architecture. Some buildings are on stilts; still others have rain gutters a foot (thirty centimeters) wide to accommodate the downpours during the rainy seasons. Some of the coastal area settlements have streets of water, like the famous European city of Venice, Italy, where boats instead of cars make up the traffic.

PARAMARIBO

Most of Suriname's traffic is on the streets of Paramaribo and the roads that radiate out from the city, either to the bauxite centers of Smalkalden and Paranam or to the airport of Zanderij. There are a few main roads that lead from other large cities to the bauxite districts.

Seventy percent of Suriname's population lives in Paramaribo or within forty miles (sixty-four kilometers) of the city. Cars travel on the left side of the road, which is customary in Great Britain and

The harbor (left) and old colonial buildings (right)

in other countries where the British have ruled (even though Britain's rule of Suriname was brief).

If you drive through Paramaribo, you find that besides cars, trucks, and taxis, the streets are crowded with bicycles, motorcycles, small buses, donkey carts loaded with food or other goods, scooters, and at the end of the day, pickup trucks loaded with men returning from fieldwork. The men each have a bird cage containing helabek birds; the birds provide company for the men, and it is a custom to take them along.

Besides motorized travel, there are many people walking, including barefoot Indians with enormous baskets of fruit on their heads. There are dogs galore. For every person in Paramaribo, there are three dogs.

There are a variety of buildings along the roads. Thatch huts are popular and environmentally sensible houses for tropical weather. Small, colorful, one-story wooden houses are built on

Some older houses are used for office space (above left) but modern office buildings (above right) have also been erected. People speaking a variety of languages are found in the busy central market.

stilts to save the residents from the rushing rain water. There are steep-roofed wooden houses such as those common in northern Europe. Here and there is a mosque, painted in a pastel color. Square telephone poles mark a trail of communication along the way.

The high humidity in the air holds odors of all kinds. The more pleasant ones are the sweet flowers of brightly blossoming trees and the rich aromas of cooking.

Many of the homes and businesses have fronts that open wide, creating a setting that is inside and outside at the same time. Cafés offer outdoor eating, and although flying insects are not a major problem, waiters bring a bucket containing an ember to keep insects away.

Like people in other countries with warm temperatures, the Surinamese take a siesta between one and three in the afternoon. Businesses close and people go home to rest.

OUTSIDE PARAMARIBO

Along the road from northern Suriname south to the Afobaka Dam near Brokopondo there are ferns as high as houses. The leaves of the paloeloe tree are 3 feet (0.9 meter) wide and 20 feet (6 meters) long. When a traveler reaches the rain forest, incredible noises are heard. It may sound like a giant festival, but the sound is of birds and frogs, seed pods thumping as they fall off the trees, and the constant drip, drip of water from the forest ceiling. The rain-forest floor is protected from both the sun and the wind, so the light is dim and the air is still. Tree trunks look like giant wire whisks with ropelike roots rising toward a winding center. A rain forest often has two hundred to three hundred kinds of trees

Rain forests cover 75 percent of Suriname.

Paramaribo

Brokopondo

A Maroon navigates the rapids on the Marowijne River.

with trunks more than 1 foot (0.3 meter) thick in 1 square mile (2.6 square kilometers).

As well as vast rain forests and the giant Afobaka Dam, Suriname has other amazing sights, including a rice plantation in northwest Suriname in the Nickerie district. This farm, called Wageningen, is the largest mechanized rice plantation in the world.

Traveling through Suriname, especially east to west, is challenging because of the many rivers that flow from deep within Suriname to the ocean. There are some bridges, but ferries often must be used to cross the waterways. Many Surinamese live along the plentiful rivers. Villages of Amerindian huts display a style of life that has been going on for centuries. In some of the villages, special fire dances are performed for tourists. Other villages provide a backdrop for the customs of their ethnic

Paramaribo

Wia Wia Nature
Preserve

Brownsberg
Nature
Park

Jaguars live in Brownsberg Nature Park.

heritage, such as Javanese dances accompanied by music from a *gamelan*, a small Indonesian orchestra of wooden xylophones and wooden or metal chimes.

Despite the huge area of wild rain forests in the country, nature preserves are maintained. An organization called Stinasu runs a large preserve called Brownsberg Nature Park. The park consists of nearly fifteen thousand acres (more than six thousand hectares) and it takes about three hours to drive there from Paramaribo. There is a full range of animals and birds—from jaguars and monkeys to macaws and toucans—and canoes can be rented for those who want to fish for walappa, patakka, or koemapari in the Brokopondo Reservoir.

Spoonbills and turtles (inset) are found in the Wia Wia Reserve.

Another preserve, the Wia Wia Reserve, lies northeast of Paramaribo and is the nesting place where five species of turtles lay their eggs. Large birds, including the wild ibis, flamingo, spoonbill, and stork, spend time in the reserve, too.

FOOD CUSTOMS

Some of the most interesting customs of different groups concern food—what people like and how they eat it. While geography has a strong historical effect on food, other customs, such as whether one eats with fingers or utensils, come from one's cultural history.

An example from one of Suriname's groups is the custom of the Javanese. Eating is a private act among these people. Women prepare a meal of rice, vegetables, and fish or poultry, plus a hot sauce. Family members come into the kitchen when they want to

Cassava is pounded and drained (left) and made into round cakes that are baked over a fire (right).

eat, gather a dish of food, and eat alone. Fathers often eat at the table in the front room, but children eat in the kitchen and women usually eat as they cook. People gather together socially for meals as they do in many parts of the world, but when they are actually eating, they excuse themselves and turn aside, eating most of the meal during those few private minutes.

Because of the wide range of ethnic groups, there are many kinds of food prepared in many ways in restaurants. Meat and vegetable dishes with names like *poi* or *nase goreng* are part of the native diet. Sometimes chicken, baked or fried, is part of a hot dish. Rice or cassava, a root vegetable similar to a potato, is a large part of most meals. Vegetables and fruits such as tomatoes, lettuce, eggplant, cabbage, mangoes, papayas, watermelons, and coconuts are available in season.

People who live and work in the city are, of course, in contact with other ethnic groups and ways of life. Their lifestyles and

choices of food and activities change more quickly than those of
people who live on farms and in villages. Nevertheless,
Surinamese in the countryside who raise food for themselves and
for selling also are affected by the people with whom they trade.

EDUCATION

Education is compulsory for children aged six to twelve.
Schooling has been mandatory since 1876, but during many years
there were not enough qualified teachers, so many children did
not go to school. After 1955 this began to change, because so
many people began to move into the cities where it was easier to
organize schools. By 1975 the number of children in school
tripled. Over 90 percent of the eligible children attended.

About half of Suriname's schools are public and the other half
are private, so about half the children attend public schools and

half attend religious and private ones. The private ones are mostly Protestant and Roman Catholic. Because religion usually runs along ethnic lines, this means that the Creoles attend Christian schools. The East Indians, most of whom are Hindus, and the Indonesian children, who are Muslims, attend public schools. These last two groups tried to set up some of their own schools, but they did not have enough money to support them, so public schools have been the main choice for the East Indian and Indonesian children.

About 19 percent of the government's budget is spent on education. Both public schools and schools sponsored by the churches are free. Schools of higher education are also free, including the University of Suriname where students can study medicine, law, economics, and social studies. There also are three technical schools and five teacher-training colleges.

At one time, 95 percent of all men and women over the age of fifteen could read and write. Few countries have had such a high literacy rate. But this rate dropped in the mid-seventies after Suriname gained its independence. Thousands of Surinamese moved to the Netherlands because they did not think the new leaders would do a good job of running the country. Many of these people were educated, so their absence made a difference in the literacy rate and in the numbers of available teachers. The literacy rate is now estimated at about 65 percent.

In 1980, Suriname started a new program for the schools. Dutch had been the language in the classroom because it was the dominant language in the country. But this was a problem for the East Indian and Indonesian children. Few of them (not even two in ten) spoke Dutch at home, so this made school more difficult than it would have been if the students had been taught in a

Because Creole children speak Dutch at home, they do well in school.

language they knew well. Many of these children dropped out of school before finishing. The new program emphasizes the importance of using other languages besides Dutch in schools and of responding to the needs of all Surinamese. The Creole children do much better in school, because many more of them (more than eight in ten) also speak Dutch at home.

One reason for this different use of language is that most of the East Indian and Indonesian people farm or live in villages. They still use their native languages, and they practice the religions and customs of their forefathers. The Creoles live in the bigger cities, where the Dutch culture has been dominant for centuries.

Meanwhile Spanish is becoming a more important language in Suriname because it is the most widely spoken language in most of South America as well as in many of the Caribbean Islands. For both political and economic purposes, Spanish is becoming more commonly spoken and taught.

All citizens aged eighteen and over can vote.

Education has helped the Surinamese find better jobs, and it has helped citizens become more informed voters. Every citizen aged eighteen years and older can vote.

WORK

Occupations for men and women in the cities, towns, and rural areas range from civil service to business and education to introducing intensive agricultural methods and family care. In the villages, however, there is work for everyone who is able. In the cities there are more people than jobs. Nearly half the employed people work for the government. They work in offices that provide services, such as handling the mail, keeping voting records, or regulating imports and exports. Some of them work on road repair or drive buses. Government workers also work to promote more tourism in Suriname.

The unemployment rate is about 33 percent, which is high. The

Surinamese who have jobs perform a wide range of work, from farming to mining to working in restaurants, banks, and food factories.

Soldiers make up another part of the workforce. Suriname has three thousand members in its military. Most belong to the infantry, although there is a small air force and a unit of navy and coastguardsmen, too. The country also has a civil police force that answers to the minister of justice.

SPORTS

Surinamese enjoy many of the sports played worldwide. Soccer, which is called football in Suriname, is popular as are golf, tennis, and horseback riding. Another sport, which now has special meaning for Suriname is swimming. In 1988 Anthony Nesty won a gold medal in the Summer Olympics in the 100-meter butterfly.

HOLIDAYS

Holidays in Suriname are both historical and religious. The ones sanctioned by the government are November 25, Independence Day; July 1, Unity Day; and February 25, Day of the Revolution, marking the day the present government took power. Religious holidays include Id al-Fitr (the end of Ramadan for Muslims) and Christmas.

HEALTH

Surinamese enjoy fairly good health, and they have reasonably good medical service. Men can expect to live to the age of sixty-

Cars drive on the left side of the road in Suriname.

seven and women to the age of seventy-two. About thirty infants die for every one thousand born. Water receives special treatment in the big cities, so it is safe to drink from the tap. Tropical diseases, such as malaria, are uncommon in Paramaribo, but in the forests, mosquitoes carry the disease.

Suriname spends only 4 percent of its budget on health, so some medicines are not available. Other expenses for people, such as welfare and social security, also receive rather small portions of the national budget—only 6.7 percent. Many of the religious groups collect money to help take care of the health and social needs in the country.

TRANSPORTATION

Highways provide more than 5,600 miles (more than 9,000 kilometers) of road, but only about one-fifth of that is in main roads. About 300 miles (483 kilometers) of roads are paved, fewer

Canoes carved from large tree trunks (top left), supply ships (top right), and ferries (below) haul both goods and people on water.

than 100 miles (160 kilometers) have gravel on them, and the others are earth, so they are dusty in the dry seasons and muddy in the rainy seasons. The main east-west road links the cities of Albina on the eastern border and Nieuw Nickerie on the west. In Paramaribo buses, taxis, motorbikes, and scooters are common. Many people ride bicycles too. There are few bridges over the many rivers in Suriname, so transportation is dominated by water travel. There are nearly 3,000 miles (4,800 kilometers) of inland waterways that people use to travel around the country. In some parts of the rivers, barges are used to haul both people and goods. Where the rivers narrow, canoes that Maroons carve from giant tree trunks offer the safest, most efficient way to travel. Paramaribo is, of course, the largest and oldest port in the country. The second main port is Moengo, and there are five others.

Railroads used to provide some transportation, but with only 103 miles (166 kilometers) of track, their usefulness was limited. Rails now are used by industry and government. None of it is for regular passenger travel.

Four airlines serve the country from the Caribbean Islands and to and from Amsterdam, Holland. The international airport is twenty-eight miles (forty-five kilometers) south of Paramaribo at Zanderij. Small planes are often the best choice for going from one place to another. Suriname Airways Ltd. flies planes in and out of all the districts, and it runs a charter service, too. There are forty usable airports in the country, although only six have hard-surfaced runways suitable for medium-sized planes.

Shipping lines in Europe, America, Japan, and Australia sail their ships to Paramaribo as part of their international tours.

A large tourist hotel in Paramaribo has air-conditioned rooms and an outdoor pool.

COMMUNICATION

People in the cities of Suriname can easily communicate with each other by telephone, telegraph, or mail. Those in most of the villages cannot communicate with distant places as easily. Telephones are sparse in some parts of the country. There are approximately thirty thousand telephones in the whole country. Mail delivery is reliable but sometimes slow. Letters mailed from outside the country, from Washington, D.C., for example, travel for ten days to two weeks. To send something by ship from the U.S. takes about two months.

Broadcast communication is varied. There are five AM radio stations, fourteen FM stations, and six television channels.

GROWTH OPPORTUNITIES

Bauxite mining and aluminum processing, plus forestry and agriculture, provide employment for most people. Changes in technology and industry have offered good opportunities for many people, especially in the cities. The Surinamese enjoy the benefits of modern life, yet many people, especially outside the cities, prefer the older ways of life.

Chapter 7

SURINAME'S PLACE
IN THE WORLD

COMMERCE AND INDUSTRY

One of the major ways that a country makes a place for itself in the world is by the products it produces and sells. Since the time that Europeans first settled Suriname, the country has had several primary exports, including sugar, cotton, coffee, gold, exotic lumber, and most recently, bauxite. Suriname's chief export in the past decades has been the ore bauxite, which was discovered early in the twentieth century. Bauxite, which looks like whole wheat bread with seeds in it, contains traces of the metal aluminum. A similar mineral, alumina, is also in bauxite. Alumina is used in the production of aluminum. On its own, it is used as an insulator in electrical installations. The country earns 70 percent of its export business from bauxite, alumina, and aluminum.

In 1916 Alcoa, the Aluminum Company of America, set up a Suriname branch called Suralco, the Suriname Aluminum Company. Mining began in the 1920s, but the production was

Suriname Aluminum Company (left) and the Afobaka Dam (right)

small until World War II. At that time, the demand for aluminum grew because of its use in building planes and other equipment for the war.

Suralco has had a great influence on the country, particularly because of the building of the Afobaka Dam across the Suriname River. This dam was built so that a huge hydroelectric power station could be constructed for processing bauxite. The dam created a lake that covered 870 square miles (2,253 square kilometers) and cost millions of dollars. It took six years of earth moving and concrete mixing to build the 1.4-mile (2.3-kilometer) main dam. The project was completed in 1964. The dam allows water to run through six powerful generators. Ninety percent of the power is pumped north to Paranam, a town 44 miles (71 kilometers) north of the lake, where the main mine is located and where bauxite is processed.

A large deposit of bauxite

While the dam was being built, many people who had farmed or had other ways of life left their homes to earn money as laborers. After working for four, five, or six years until the dam was finished, many workers wanted to continue to work for money instead of returning to their old ways of life. Some people moved to the cities looking for other kinds of jobs. This effect on the workforce was one result of the mining venture.

Another change was caused by the lake, named the Dr. W.J. van Blommestein Meer (lake) after the Dutch man who first had the idea in the 1940s. The name of the lake is now sometimes shortened to Van Blommestein Lake. As the lake slowly formed behind the dam, it flooded forty-three villages, whose inhabitants had been moved away. Thousands of animals were left to escape if they could or simply to drown. An international group, the Society for the Prevention of Cruelty to Animals, sponsored an

Monkeys were saved from the flooding waters caused by the Afobaka Dam.

American named John Walsh. He was to lead a crew of workers to save as many animals as possible.

Walsh knew that larger animals, such as jaguars, deer, and tapirs, could swim up to 1.8 miles (2.9 kilometers), but some of the small monkeys and squirrels could manage not much more than 10 yards (9 meters). As the water rose, the animals would either find themselves on islands that became smaller and smaller separated by greater and greater distances or be left clinging to the tops of trees. Many who did not drown would starve to death.

Traveling in dugout canoes 15 to 30 feet (4.5 to 9 meters) long, carved from Wana trees, Walsh and his crew paddled the flooded area, saving a total of ten thousand animals. To preserve the balance of nature, they had to save poisonous snakes and spiny rats as well as lizards, agoutis (South American rodents, much

Agoutis (above) and piranhas (right)

like rabbits), anteaters, and sloths. They saved large animals, such as deer, armadillos, peccaries, land tortoises, and one capybara. And the men saved small animals, including snakes, geckos (there are three hundred species), large centipedes, toads the size of coffee cans, and a termite nest that Walsh said was as big as an oven.

Among the dangers they faced were the piranha fish with their razor-sharp teeth. The presence of these fish explains why swimming is not more popular in Suriname. One of Walsh's crew sat on a dock dangling his foot in the water, and suddenly his little toe—bone, muscle, and all—was sheared off by the small but fast fish. Piranhas, which measure a mere ten inches (twenty-five centimeters) in length and have blood-red eyes, kill more humans than any other water animal.

None of the crew was attacked by snakes, but there were

The dangerous bushmaster

several poisonous snakes in the area, from little ones to the widely feared bushmaster, a 12-foot (3.7-meter) pit viper that will go out of its way to strike a human. The bite usually kills within an hour. Despite the sacrifices made for bauxite, the mineral has allowed Suriname to compete on the international market and earn money for its needs.

AGRICULTURE

Agriculture is important to many people within Suriname. Families with small plots have been able to feed themselves and sell extra crops to others.

Of course, large-scale farms grow food exclusively for export. One plant that grows well in Suriname because of the long, warm growing season and the wet earth is rice. It is grown for domestic use and it also is the chief agricultural export.

Suriname's location on the globe has made it ideal for growing a number of tropical plants, including sugarcane, palm trees (for the oil that is pressed from their fruit), and bananas, which also are very important exports. In addition, the country sells coconuts, plantains, citrus fruits, and vegetables.

Both bananas, which are grown on plantations (above), and
rice (below)—more than seventy varieties—are major exports.

Freshly caught fish for sale in the market

FISHING

With a long seacoast, it is no surprise that fishing is an
important part of Suriname's economy. Commercial fishing
provides a good portion of Suriname's income. Saltwater fish and
crabs as well as freshwater fish from the many rivers are captured
and sold. Shrimp has long been the most important fishing
export.

FORESTRY

Because most of Suriname's land is covered with rain forests,
lumber has been a resource that has been sold since the
Europeans' first successful settlement. There are typical hardwood
trees in Suriname that could be found in many places on the
earth, but of special interest are the so-called tropical trees that
have special features. Some of them, like teak, have great

A giant teak tree

resistance to humidity and are strong. Others are very flexible and lightweight, such as balata. Products from this tree, a relative of the rubber tree, have many uses in manufacturing, including as a covering for golf balls. The sale of these trees brought a lot of money to Suriname. From 1909 to 1913 it was the country's chief export—more important than gold.

Along with specialty woods sold for furniture, flooring, or veneer, common woods are sold for fuel and industrial uses.

SURINAME'S FUTURE

While it is not possible to predict a precise future for a country, an examination of what has gone on in the politics and economics of the country offers some things to think about.

Like many other countries in the world, Suriname often has had a single major export, such as bauxite, gold, cotton, or sugar. Therefore, the economy of the country is heavily influenced by the success of the product on the international market. When things are going well, the country prospers, but when the product is no longer wanted or the price drops because there is too much of it, the country is in trouble.

Another disadvantage to having a single main export is that if the resource is used up, the country suffers if it does not find another export, or another way to bring money into the country— quickly. Some experts believe Suriname's bauxite will be exhausted by the year 2010. Perhaps other deposits will be discovered, but if not, Suriname's economy will face another crisis.

A third problem with a single-product economy is that the country often has to make extraordinary sacrifices to deliver the product. One example is money that Suriname lost when a gold-mining company built a poorly constructed railroad and the country was stuck with unending repairs.

Even though Suriname gets money from exporting its resources, it has been dependent on the Netherlands and the United States for additional aid. During the sixty-year gap between the time that the slaves were freed and World War II began, Suriname borrowed nearly 40 percent of its budget.

Suriname's effort to rely more on itself and less on foreign investors has been spoiled repeatedly by political problems— rebellions by people in the interior of the country, unexpected decisions made by distrusted military personnel, or poor management of the country by elected officials. These problems make it difficult for companies to conduct business within the country, and they make foreign countries and businesses leery of dealing with Suriname.

Suriname's participation in the Caribbean community is growing, as seems appropriate to their common history and their economic and geographical interests. Perhaps local involvement will benefit Suriname in the long run. The country's dealings with Cuba, which has a Communist dictator, makes some other governments uncomfortable, but there are many economic and political changes occurring in that part of the world. Who knows what the next few years will bring?

Another growing pressure that Suriname shares with other countries in the rain-forest belt is the worry of cutting down too much of the forest and affecting the earth's atmosphere. This situation, where a country needs to respond to global environmental concerns in the development of its economy, is relatively new. The international debates over fishing rights have been similar.

Besides the economic future of the country, the political and social futures also are uncertain. Since Suriname gained independence from the Netherlands, there have been some years of peace with the new government; but, so far, these do not compensate for the many years of problems, greed, and disruption.

Furthermore, the emigration of citizens to other countries, especially to the Netherlands, has been remarkable. Paramaribo has been stripped of much of its former character by a sharp decline in population. Government mismanagement and confusion contribute to bad feelings among citizens. Some people think

Sooner or later everyone visits the central market in Paramaribo.

The challenges facing Suriname are large and the future for these youngsters is unpredictable.

independence from the Netherlands was a bad idea. The power of Desi Bouterse is still a factor, and many people do not trust him and do not believe he has the best interests of the country in mind.

The once peaceful and prosperous Suriname has entered an era where both its present and its future are uncertain. Dissatisfaction is high among many citizens. Perhaps the only likely future for Suriname is change. Its form and consequences are unknown, but the years since independence have been largely restless. The leaders have not laid the groundwork for a safe and steady future. What actually happens will be of interest to many countries in the Caribbean and South America and to all of the countries worldwide that have social and economic connections to Suriname.

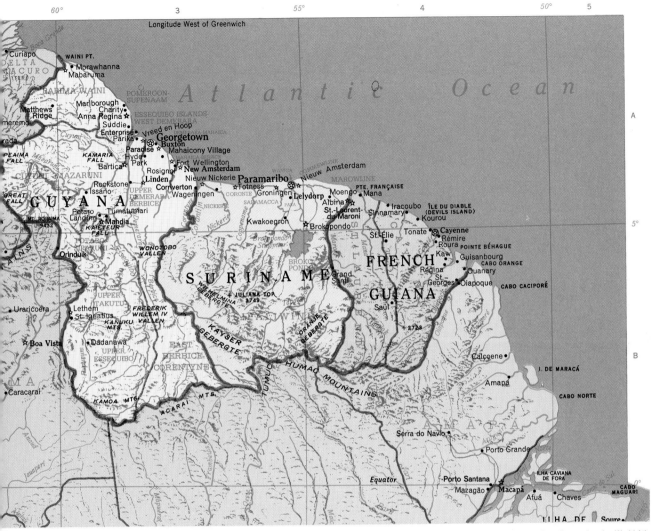

Map from Comprehensive World Atlas,
© 1995 by Rand McNally, 94-S-267

MAP KEY

Albina	A4
Blommestein Meer, *lake*	B3, B4
Brokopondo	A4
Brokopondo, *province*	A3, A4, B3, B4
Charlottenburg	A4
Commewijne, *province*	A3, A4, B4
Coppename, *river*	A3, B3
Coronie, *province*	A3
Courantyne, *river*	A3, B3
Grand Sant	B4
Groningen	A3
Joliana Top, *peak*	B3
Kayser Gebergte, *mountain range*	B3
Kwakoegron	A3
Maroni, *river*	A4, B4
Marowijne, *province*	A4, B3, B4
Moengo	A4
Nickerie, *province*	A3, B3
Nickerie, *river*	A3, B3
Nieuw Amsterdam	A3
Nieuw Nickerie	A3
Oranje Gebergte, *mountain range*	B3, B4
Para, *province*	A3
Paramaribo	A3
Paranam	A3
Pointe Francaise	A4
Saramacca, *province*	A3, B3
Suriname, *province*	A3
Tapanahony, *river*	B3, B4
Totness	A3
Wageningen	A3
Wilhelmina Gebergte, *mountain range*	B3

MINI-FACTS AT A GLANCE

GENERAL INFORMATION

Official Name: *Republiek Suriname* (Republic of Suriname)

Capital: Paramaribo

Government: Suriname is a multiparty republic with one legislative house, the National Assembly, of 51 members. National Assembly members are elected by universal adult (over 18 years) suffrage for a five-year term. The president is the head of state and of the government, and appoints a Council of Ministers that is responsible to the legislative council (*Staten van Surinam*). The vice president also serves as prime minister. The judicial power rests with the Court of Justice, whose members are nominated by the president.
Before 1975 the country was called Dutch Guiana. For administrative purposes Suriname is divided into nine districts and one town district, Paramaribo.

Religion: There is no official religion in Suriname. People are free to follow the religion of their choice. The Amerindian religion centers on *animism,* a belief in many kinds of spirits. The majority of Asiatic people are Hindus and Muslims; the Creole group is mostly Roman Catholic but some Creoles follow the traditional religion known in Suriname as Winti. Other Christian denominations are Protestant, Lutheran, Dutch Reformed, Methodist, African Methodist Episcopal, Baptist, Seventh-Day Adventist, Jehovah's Witness, and Pentecostal. There is a small Jewish population.

Ethnic Composition: Suriname's population is a mixture of a number of ethnic groups that have preserved their own culture, religion, and language. The major ethnic groups are Hindustanis (Indians), Creoles, Javanese, Maroons, Amerindians, Chinese, Europeans, and Lebanese. Amerindians are Surinam's original inhabitants; major groups are Arawak, Carib, Trio, Akoerio, and Wajana. The Maroons, also sometimes called Bush Negroes, are descended from African slaves.

Language: The official language is Dutch, but English also is spoken widely. A local language, Sranan Tongo or "Taki-Taki," a mixture of Dutch, West African, English, and Portuguese, is used. Hindi, Javanese, and several Chinese, Amerindian, and African languages and dialects are spoken. Sarnami Hindustani is the most widely spoken Hindi dialect, while the Surinam Javanese, with many Dutch and Sranan Tongo words, is the language of Indonesians. Creoles speak Surinaams-Nederlands, a language similar to Dutch. Spanish is becoming important for both political and economic purposes. German and Portuguese are spoken by small numbers of people.

National Flag: Adopted in 1975, the flag has five horizontal stripes of green, white, red, white, and green. The middle red band is broad with a yellow star at the center, symbolizing unity, sacrifice, and a golden future. Red is a symbol of love and progressive spirit, white symbolizes justice and freedom, and the green stands for the hope for progress.

National Emblem: The basic design for the national emblem dates from the 17th century. It consists of two Amerindian warriors flanking an oval shield that is vertically divided into two halves. A sailing ship and a palm tree appear on each half. A five-pointed star is displayed in the center diamond. The shield and the Amerindians stand on a scroll proclaiming the national motto: *Justitia, Pietas, Fides,* "Justice, Piety, Faith."

National Anthem: The *Surinaams Volkslied* (National Anthem) begins "God zij met ons Suriname" ("God be with our Suriname")

National Calendar: Gregorian

Money: Suriname guilder (Sf) is the national currency. In 1993, 1 Suriname guilder was worth $0.56 in United States currency.

Membership in International Organizations: Caribbean Common Market (CARICOM); International Bauxite Association (IBA); Inter-American Development Bank (IDB); International Monetary Fund (IMF); Nonaligned Movement (NAM); Organization of American States (OAS); United Nations (UN)

Weights and Measures: The metric system is in use.

Population: 453,000 (1994 estimates); density 7 persons per sq. mi. (3 persons per sq km); 50 percent urban, 50 percent rural

Cities:
Paramaribo	192,109
Nieuw Nickerie	6,078
Meerzorg	5,355
Marienburg	3,633

(Population based on 1980 census, except Paramaribo, which is based on the 1988 estimate.)

GEOGRAPHY

Border: The southern border meets Brazil; Guyana is to the west; and French Guiana is to the east. The Atlantic Ocean forms the entire northern boundary.

Coastline: 226 mi. (364 km) along the Atlantic Ocean

Land: The coastal plains, mostly at sea level, extend in the north. Covering about 15 percent of the total land, these plains with partially fertile soils, are the most densely populated region in the country. The swampy and marshy plains have been drained at places to make land available for farming. The swampy areas have some beach ridges and mud banks, deposits from slow-moving rivers in their delta stage. South of these are the slightly elevated fanlike plains in the east central and a high grassland plateau in the southwest. The largely unexplored mountainous rain forests rise gradually and cover about 75 percent of the country. The Van Asch Van Wijk range in the central part of Suriname runs southward to the Tumac-Humac Mountains on the Brazilian border.

Suriname has territorial disputes with neighboring Guyana over 6,000 sq. mi. (15,000 sq km) of land, and also with French Guiana over land to the east of the Litani River.

Highest Point: Juliana Top, 4,200 ft. (1,280 m)

Lowest Point: Sea level

Rivers: Rivers form Suriname's eastern, western, and southern borders. All major rivers, the Suriname, the Courantyne, the Nickerie, the Coppename, the Saramacca, the Commewijne, and the Maroni, flow towards the Atlantic Ocean in the north. Suriname's numerous rivers are joined by a complicated system of man-made channels to allow navigation from one river to another. Few rivers have bridges; often ferries must be used to cross the waterways.

The Afobaka Dam, built across the Suriname River in the east-central part of the country, generates electricity used for processing bauxite at Paranam. Formed behind the dam is the 870 sq. mi. (2,253 sq km) wide man-made Blommestein Lake, the country's largest lake. After completion the lake flooded forty-three villages whose inhabitants and animals had been moved away.

Forests: More than 75 percent of the total land area is under forests; rain forests with some 1,000 species of trees are dominant. Special tropical trees such as teak (a strong wood with great resistance to humidity) and balata (famous for its flexibility and light weight) are exported. The hardwood trees have many uses in manufacturing, furniture, flooring, and sports. Some large forest areas have been left alone by developers for the study of medicinal plants and other research. Tropical shrubs include hibiscus, bougainvillea, and oleander. Suriname has about 4,000 species of ferns; at some places the ferns are as high as houses. The paloeloe tree has leaves that are 3 ft. (0.9 m) wide and 20 ft. (6 m) long. There are a number of flowers in Suriname, but water lilies and orchids are the best known.

The *Stinasu* organization runs a 15,000-acre (6,000-hectare) nature preserve called Brownsberg Nature Park, which is full of animals, birds, and fish. The Wia Wia Reserve has five species of turtles, and large birds such as wild ibis, flamingos, spoonbills, and storks.

Wildlife: Suriname has 13 nature parks and 3 nature preserves. Some 600 species of birds and 150 species of mammals, including deer and monkeys, inhabit the rain forests. The largest mammal is the tapir; others are the manatee, jaguar, ocelot, agouti (South American rabbit), tortoise, leopard, zebra, tiger, sloth, anteater, armadillo, and capybara or bush pig. Suriname law protects marine turtles of various species. Reptiles include iguana, caiman, and numerous snakes ranging from small ones to the 12-ft. (3.7-m) long bushmaster. A number of insects are found in Suriname, including large centipedes and spiders. Piranha fish with their razor-sharp teeth abound in the rivers; they kill more humans than any water animal.

Climate: Suriname receives plentiful and nearly constant rainfall. There are four main seasons, two wet and two dry. The long rainy season is from April to August followed by a long, dry season from August to November. A shorter and less wet rainy season runs from December to February and a shorter dry season from February to March. The daytime temperatures vary from 73° F. (23° C) to 88° F. (31° C). At night the range is 66° F (19° C) to 81° F. (27° C). The northeastern trade winds blow in from the sea all year and have a moderating effect on temperatures. The annual rainfall ranges between 76 in. to 95 in. (192 cm to 241 cm), but is highest in the southern mountains. The humidity is high throughout the year in most of the country.

Greatest Distance: North to South: 285 mi. (459 km)
East to West: 280 mi. (451 km)

Area: 63,037 sq. mi. (163,265 sq km)

ECONOMY AND INDUSTRY

Agriculture: Less than 1 percent of the land is available for cultivation. During the Dutch occupation swamps were transformed into plantations for cash crops by building dikes to keep water away. Rice is the largest export crop; about 75 percent of the agricultural area is under rice cultivation. Coffee, sugarcane, palm kernels (for oil), and cocoa also are grown for export. Citrus fruits, bananas, plantains, manioc, yams, and vegetables are produced chiefly for local use. The Wageningen Farm in the Nickerie District is the largest mechanized rice plantation in the world. These large-scale farms grow food crops exclusively for export.

Fishing: Fishing is an important part of the country's economy. Some 350 species of fish are found in the coastal and inland waters. Freshwater fish like walappa, patakka, and koemapari, and saltwater fish and crabs are caught and exported. Shrimp is the most important fishing export product.

Mining: Suriname is one of the world's leading producers of bauxite. The bauxite industry is the primary mining activity, dominating both the mining and the manufacturing sectors. Large bauxite deposits exist at Smalkalden and Paranam. The ore is exported mainly to the United States. There are also extensive deposits of iron ore and reserves of manganese, copper, nickel, platinum, gold, and kaolin. Petroleum-bearing sand was discovered in the Saramacca District and some offshore oil reserves also have been found.

Manufacturing: Bauxite refining and smelting is the principal manufacturing activity. Locally processed alumina and aluminum accounts for about 80 percent of the total export revenue. An industrial zone near Paramaribo produces clothing, footwear, foodstuffs, domestic utensils, furniture, and some consumer goods. Other manufacturing includes food processing, cigarettes, beverages, and construction material.

Energy is derived primarily from imported petroleum. There is considerable potential for developing hydroelectric power. The Afobaka hydroelectric dam provides electricity for bauxite smelting.

Transportation: The 103 mi. (166 km) of single-track railway is chiefly used by industry and government, but is not in use for regular passenger travel. Out of 5,600 mi. (9,012 km) of roads, less than one-third are paved; the unpaved roads are dusty in the dry seasons and muddy in the rainy seasons. The international airport is located south of Paramaribo at Zanderij. Suriname Airways Limited provides service to all districts and runs a charter service too. Internal waterways are the most important means of transportation; Suriname has 3,000 mi. (4,828 km) of navigable waterways. Barges are used to haul both people and goods. Canoes offer an efficient way to travel in the narrow rivers. Paramaribo is the chief port, followed by Moengo; there are five more ports along the coast. Local city transportation consists of cars, trucks, taxis, bicycles, motorcycles, small buses, donkey carts, scooters, and pick-up trucks.

Communication: People in cities have easy access to telephone, telegraph, and mail. AM and FM radio and television channels provide news and entertainment. Newspapers are published in Dutch, Chinese, and English. In the early 1990s there was one radio receiver per 1.6 persons; one television set per 9.4 persons, and one telephone per 15 persons.

Trade: The chief imports are machinery, transport equipment, petroleum and lubricants, foodstuff, cars and motorcycles, raw materials, and semi-manufactured goods. The major import sources are Brazil, the United States, the Netherlands, Japan, the United Kingdom, Trinidad and Tobago, and Netherland Antilles. The chief export items are alumina, aluminum, shrimp, bananas, sugar, cotton, coffee, gold, wood and wood products, and bauxite. The major export destinations are Brazil, Norway, the Netherlands, the United States, Japan, the United Kingdom, and France.

EVERYDAY LIFE

Health: Health conditions in general are good, as are medical services. Drinking water from the tap is safe in big cities. Mosquitoes carry malaria in the forests, but cities are almost free of this disease. Tuberculosis and syphilis, once the chief causes of death, are under control. Modern health facilities are financed by Dutch and European funds. Life expectancy stands at 67 years for males and 72 years for females. Infant mortality rate at 30 per 1,000 is moderately high. In the early 1990s there was one physician per 1,350 persons and one hospital bed per 212 persons.

Education: Education is compulsory for children between six and twelve years of age. Secondary education lasts for seven years. About one-half of the schools are public and the other half are private, sponsored by religious organizations. All schools are free. Most Creoles attend Catholic or Protestant mission schools, but most Hindus and Muslims attend public schools. University education also is free; the main faculties are medicine, law, economics, and social studies. There are three technical schools and five teacher-training colleges. Adult education is emphasized by the government. In the early 1990s the literacy rate was about 95 percent, one of the highest in the world, but in the 1990s it is estimated to be 65 percent.

Holidays:
New Year's Day, January 1
Revolution Day, February 25
Labor Day, May 1
National Unity Day, July 1
Independence Day, November 25
Christmas, December 25
Boxing Day, December 26
Religious holidays such as Holi, Good Friday, Easter, and Id al-Fitr fall on different dates each year.

Culture: The country's culture is reflected in pottery, clothing, poetry, music, wood carving, calabash carving, dance, music, and storytelling. The main public library is at the Suriname Cultural Center in Paramaribo. The Suriname State Museum is the largest museum in the country.

Society: Both Amerindians and Maroons have stayed in the forested interior of the country for generations. Ritual life is the centerpiece of these communities. The birth of a girl is an occasion of special celebration among the Maroons as the family line is carried through the women. Sometimes a Maroon man has more than one wife, and divorce is quite common. The Maroon men and women carve wood or the thick skin of the gourdlike calabash fruit and give away their art objects as gifts of love. Men customarily carry a birdcage with helabek birds with them everywhere. In cities the Surinamese take a siesta between one and three in the afternoon; businesses close and people go home to rest.

Dress: The Javanese women dress in *batik* fabric. They also use this cloth to wrap around their heads and to make sarongs, dresses that wrap around the body. Maroon women wear kerchiefs on their heads and long calico dresses. They embroider capes and neckerchiefs in brilliant colors and patterns. The Saramaccan women refer to their skirts of simple rectangles by an event that occurred when the skirt was sewn. These women's skirts are a way to track history of the person, and that of her village and their culture.

Housing: Small colorful one-story wooden houses are on stilts to save the residents from rushing rainwater. Some houses have a wide gutter to accommodate the heavy rains. Some coastal areas have streets of water with boat traffic. In rural areas people live in thatched huts that are environmentally sensible for the tropical weather. In cities many buildings have roofs that rise steeply in the Dutch architectural fashion.

Food: Rice and cassava are the staples in Suriname. Surinamese meals include tomatoes, lettuce, eggplants, cabbage, mangoes, papayas, watermelons, coconuts, chicken, and some fish. *Poi* and *nase goreng* are native dishes. Baked or fried chicken is generally part of a hot dish. A Javanese meal consists of rice, vegetables, fish or poultry, and hot sauce. Fathers often eat alone at the table while Javanese women and children eat in the kitchen in seclusion. In Paramaribo cafés and restaurants offer outdoor eating.

Recreation: *Seketi* are the Maroon popular songs composed by nearly everyone. Javanese dances are accompanied by a *gamelan,* a small Indonesian orchestra of wooden xylophones and chimes.

Social Welfare: Social welfare is largely dependent on the private initiative of the community and the religious organizations. The government subsidizes orphanages.

IMPORTANT DATES

2000 B.C.—American Indians have discovered agriculture, pottery, and weaving; the Arawak and the Carib are the main tribes of Guiana

A.D. 1400—The Carbis, who maintain sea trade along the Guiana coast, have almost wiped out the Arawaks

1498—Christopher Columbus sights the land that is now Suriname

1651—British explorers build the first permanent settlement

1662—England's Charles II gives the land of Suriname to Lord Willoughby and Earl Laurens Hide

1667—The Dutch seize the Suriname region from the British; the British recapture it, but give it back to the Dutch in the Treaty of Breda

1674—The Treaty of Westminister confirms authority of the Netherlands over Suriname

1735—Moravian Brethren begin preaching among the Maroons

1787—Roman Catholics begin missionary work with the slaves

1791—The population of Suriname is about 49,000; one-fifth of the people live in Paramaribo

1799-1802—Suriname is under British control

1804—Suriname once again comes under British rule

1814—Slavery is outlawed in all Dutch colonies

1816—British rule ends in Suriname

1853—Chinese laborers are brought to Suriname to work on plantations

1863—Slavery in Suriname is abolished by the Dutch; laborers are brought in from India and Indonesia to work on plantations

1866—The Dutch impose The Suriname Government Order plan

1873-1916—Some thirty-four thousand East Indians are brought to Suriname as contract workers

1876—Education becomes compulsory for schoolchildren

1880—The gold rush begins (ends in 1910)

1890-1939—More than thirty-three thousand Indonesians are brought to Suriname as contract workers

1916—The Suriname Aluminum Company (Suralco) is set up

1930—The Netherlands and Suriname decide against contract immigration

1939—The Dutch mining company Billiton sets up operation in Suriname

1945—Queen Wilhelmina of the Netherlands initiates reforms in Suriname

1948—Suriname holds its first full elections; the Netherlands begins to provide development aid to Suriname

1954—The Dutch government changes the administrative setup of Suriname from a colony to a territory; Suriname gets autonomy in its internal affairs

1958—Elections are held

1961—The Nationalist Republican Party (PNR) is established

1964—The Afobaka Dam is completed; as an associate member of the European Economic Community (EEC) Suriname starts receiving development funds from the EEC

1967—Elections are held

1969—The Foundation for Nature Preservation is established

1975—Suriname becomes an independent republic under a new constitution; some 90 percent of school-age children are enrolled in schools

1976—The government announces that Spanish will become the nation's principal working language

1977—National elections are held

1980—A violent army coup deposes Prime Minister Henck Arron; a state of emergency is declared; Desi Bouterse, a military sergeant takes charge of the country; schools adopt a policy to encourage languages other than Dutch as a medium of instruction; the University of Suriname is renamed as the Anton de Kom University

1981—Petroleum-bearing sand is discovered in the Saramacca District

1982—Desi Bouterse seizes power from Dr. Henk Chin A. Sen and the civilian government; the Netherlands breaks diplomatic relations with Suriname; the United States and the Netherlands suspend aid to Suriname; the government announces an action program to encourage small-scale industries, establishment of industrial parks, and rural electrification

1983—Bauxite workers go on strike; Suriname breaks diplomatic relations with Cuba; Brazil and Suriname sign trade agreements; the Progressive Workers' and Farm Laborers' Union (PALU) and Revolutionary People's Party (RVP) form a coalition government

1985—A new constitution is written

1986—Guerrilla attacks disrupt the country's bauxite production

1987—General elections are held for the National Assembly; a new constitution is approved by 93 percent of the votes; Ramsewak Shankar is elected president

1988—The National Assembly elects a president and a vice president

1990—Bouterse resigns as commander in chief of the armed forces; President Ramsewak Shankar is ousted in a bloodless coup; power is seized by Ivan Graanoogst; the Netherlands suspends development aid to Suriname

1991—The Military Council is abolished; general elections are held

1992—Bouterse resigns again as commander in chief of the armed forces; work begins on South America's first crude oil cross-country pipeline which is 34 mi. (55 km) long and 14 in. (36 cm) wide; this pipeline will deliver crude oil to the Tout Lui Faut terminal near the capital

IMPORTANT PEOPLE

Errol Alibux, prime minister in 1984

Henck Arron (1936-   ), a Surinamese of Creole origin; elected prime minister in 1973; he was ousted in an army coup in 1980

Dr. Ingenieur W.J. van Blommestein, the Dutch engineer who in the 1940s first thought of building the Afobaka Dam

Lieutenant Colonel Desi Bouterse (1945-   ), leader of the army coup in 1980

Ronnie Brunswijk, a Maroon leader of a group called the Jungle Commando

Cyriel Daal (? -1982), a trade union leader; murdered by the army in 1982

Johan Ferrier (1910-   ), the first president

Ivan Graanoogst, an army commander who took over after a 1990 coup

Nola Hatterman, artist and painter; she is honored as a great painter; Suriname's Painters' Institute is named after her

Anton de Kom (1946?-   ), a Surinamese of Creole origin; wrote a book about slavery in Suriname

Ismene Krishnadadh, writer; writes mostly for children; won Suriname's national literary prize in 1993

Kwaku, a slave leader of the Maroons; his statue is in Paramaribo

Jaggernath Lachmon, a Surinamese of East Indian origin; worked with Henck Arron to prepare Suriname for independence

I. Fred Ramdat Misier, interim president after 1982 army coup

Henry Neyjorst, an economist; prime minister after the 1982 coup

Marta Tjoe Nie, writer and poet

Mark Plotkin, the vice president for plant conservation at the Washington, D.C.-based organization, Conservation International; does research by gathering medicinal plants in the rain forests of Suriname with the help of Trio Indian shamans or wise men, and processes them in the United States for different medicinal use

Robin Raveles, poet; has written about Surinamese nationalism; his "One Tree" poem has become an unofficial national song for the country

Dr. Henk Chin A. Sen (1934-   ), a leader of the Nationalist Republican Party (PNR); was appointed by President Ferrier to head a civilian group at the time of emergency in 1980; he later replaced President Ferrier; was dismissed by the Military Council in 1982

Ramsewak Shankar, political leader; became president after the 1987 elections; belongs to the Indian Progressive Reform Party (VHP)

Michael Slory, poet; writes in Dutch and Sranan Tongo

Willy Soemita, an Indonesian Peasant's Party (KTPI) leader

John Gabriel Stedman (1744-97), British soldier; arrived in Suriname in 1773; kept a journal describing the terrible treatment of the slaves by the Europeans

Shrini Vasi, poet

Compiled by Chandrika Kaul

INDEX

Page numbers that appear in boldface type indicate illustrations

Opposite page: The Suriname River runs through the rain forest.

124

rivers, 7, 10-11, **10,** 12, **34,** 82, **82,** 93, 96, 112

Roman Catholic Church, 38, 60, 61, **61,** 62, 87, 110, 117

St. Peter and Paul Cathedral, **61**

Saramacca, 10, 68-69, 74, 114, 119

Saramacca River, 11, 112

Saramaccan language, 53, 116

Saramaccans, **58, 68, 70**

Sarnami Hindustani, 53, 111

Second Anglo-Dutch War, 21

Sen, Henk Chin A., 44, 45, 119, 121

Shankar, Ramsewak, 46, 48-49, 120, 121

slavery, 13, 23-27, **23,** 29-30, **29,** 51, 61, 117, 118

Slory, Michael, 56, 121

sloths, **17**

Smalkalden, 77, 114

snakes, 99-100, **100**

social welfare, 117

society, 116

Society for the Prevention of Cruelty to Animals, 97-98

Soemita, Willy, 46, 121

South America, 7

Spanish, 19, 54-55, 111

Spanish Inquisition, 62

Spanish language, 88

sports, 90

square miles, 8, 113

Sranan Tongo, 52, 53, 54, 56, 110, 111

Stedman, John Gabriel, 25-26, 27, 121

Stinasu, 83, 113

Supreme Council, 46

Suralco, 95-96, 118

Surinaams-Nederlands, 54, 111

Suriname (district), 10, 74, 119

Suriname, University of, 87, 119

Suriname Cultural Center, 116

Suriname Government Order Plan, 35, 118

Suriname Progressive People's Party (PVS), 38

Suriname River, 11, 68, 96, 112, **122**

Suriname State Museum, 116

Surinen, 65

tapirs, **16,** 17

television, 94, 115

tidal marsh, **12**

Tobago, 115

Tout Lui Faut, 120

trade, 9, 10, 22, 95-100, 104, 115

transportation, 11, **11,** 77-78, 91, **91, 92,** 93, 114-115

Trinidad, 115

Trio Indians, 17-18, **18,** 53

Tumac-Humac Mountains, 9, 112

United Hindu Party (VHP), 39

United Kingdom, 115

United Nations (UN), 111

United States, 46, 104, 115, 119

Unity Day, 90

Van Asch Van Wijk Range, 9, 112

van Blommestein, W. J. (Ingenieur), 120

Vasi, Shrini, 56, 121

Venezuela, 7, 8

Voltaire, François-Marie, 26-27, **26**

Wageningen Farm, 82, 114

Wajana, 53

Walsh, John, 98

"Wan Bon" (Raveles), 41

water transportation, 11, **11,** 13, **92,** 93, 115

weights, 111

Westminister, Treaty of, 117

Wia Wia Reserve, 84, **84,** 113

wildlife, 14, **16,** 17, **17,** 71, 83, **83,** 84, **84,** 97-100, **98, 99, 100,** 113

Wilhelmina, Queen, 37, **38, 40,** 118

Wilhelmina Mountains, 9

Willoughby, Francis (Lord), 20, 117

Winti, 60, 110

women, **5, 36, 50,** 56, 58, **58,** 59, **59, 68,** 70-71, **72, 73, 75, 76,** 84, 116

yagurundis, **16,** 17

Zanderij, 77, 93, 114

About the Author

Carolyn Lieberg is a writer and editor in Princeton, New Jersey, where she works for the Carnegie Foundation for the Advancement of Teaching. She has been editor of two magazines, including a children's history magazine, *The Goldfinch*, for the State Historical Society of Iowa, which won the Educational Press Association's Golden Lamp in 1990. She has published fiction and nonfiction for children and adults. She has a graduate degree in writing from the University of Iowa and has an abiding interest in history and geography. She extends her appreciation to her daughters, Adria and Rachel, for their support, and to Craig Johnson, friend and librarian, for his generous assistance.